God Magnet

#humanattractsGod

You are a Walking Revival
Waiting to Happen

Mandy Adendorff

5 Fold Media
Visit us at www.5foldmedia.com

ISBN: 978-1-942056-05-8
Library of Congress Control Number: 2015939124

Endorsements

I remember the first time Mandy Adendorff prayed for us without knowing our circumstances, and how God blessed us! I was certain that God had extraordinarily anointed my new friend. Over the years, I've come to know Mandy's heart for the Lord and her joy in seeing renewal come through Jesus Christ to so many. *God Magnet* is a blend of Mandy's God stories and teachings that will lead the reader through a journey of God's beauty and plan for us. It will empower the reader to experience Christ's extraordinary anointing through being open to what He has for us. I plan to share this book with many in my church and highly recommend others do the same. Prepare your wineskin to be stretched for the precious truths contained in this book!

-Pastor Annmarie Boulay
Wintonbury Church, CT

God Magnet made my heart sing! Like the song a robin releases after returning to a familiar place at spring after a long winter, Mandy's beautiful articulation of the profound reality of God's indwelling presence in His children melts the frost of performance-driven Christianity. It introduces the reader to the newness of life that accompanies the privilege of housing God's presence as living temples. Mandy's words paint a beautiful picture of the invitational nature of His presence that is both glorious in its vision and practical in its application. *God Magnet* does not contain lofty ideas that are unattainable but rather a compelling vision of the Christian life that I long for as a son of God. I believe windows of revelation will be opened as people read this book and the fresh aroma and warmth of spring will enter the heart desiring more of His presence.

-Leroy Case
Itinerant and Pastor, CT

3

God Magnet brings some amazing insight into understanding personal growth. Mandy's keen perception into spiritual matters that trap many in dark spiritual depression reveals how these traps can be broken by realignment to God's vision of who we are.

God Magnet is a brilliant compilation of personal experiences as seen through the creative artist lens; it should speak volumes to those who feel untouched by the sovereignty of the Holy Spirit and His guidance. *God Magnet* could be used for both personal and small group study. Enjoy the revelation as you travel through its pages.

-Rev. Mark Dornbusch
Lead Pastor, New Hope Christian Center, Oak View, CA

God Magnet! My first thought was, "This is really an unusual title for a book." But then I reminded myself that Mandy Adendorff is not your usual, run-of-the-mill person. She is full of God-life. Her inquiring mind, vivid imagination, and thirsty spirit are alive with the presence, power, and purpose of the Creator. Mandy brings a fresh and exciting perspective to Scripture and life through her art, writing, and teaching ministry. Simply stated, she is herself a God magnet and capably declares that God made all of us with the ability to attract Him.

Mandy brings to the pages of this wonderful book her experience as a South African girl growing up in apartheid Africa, the eye of an accomplished painter and artist who is able to see the colors and shadows of life, and her Jewish DNA that provides an amazing insight into the Old Testament Law and the tabernacle.

This book will stretch you and challenge your thinking. Be prepared to enlarge your world, your faith, and your fruitfulness as a servant of King Jesus. Mandy will introduce you to a boundless God who is real and speaks to us individually. A new world of possibilities is within your reach. Discover how to increase your capacity for God's presence. Become a God magnet.

-Dr. Dale A. Fife
Author of *The Secret Place: A Prophetic Invitation to Intimacy with God*
Founder and president of Mountain Top Global Ministries, USA

Mandy Adendorff is an amazing artist, teacher, wife, and mother. She has a way of taking the truth of God's Word and putting it into language that will touch the hearts of those who read and hear. *God Magnet* will draw the reader into a greater knowledge of the holy. Ordinary Christians will be discipled by the truths in this book.

-**Pastor Barbara G. Lachance**
USA, barbara@generationalsolutionsllc.com

It is awesome to think of ourselves as "magnets" of God's presence. That God, the Creator of the universe, wants us to deliberately position ourselves to draw in His presence—wow! I remember the day when revelation came to me that through my second birth and through my relationship with God I have now become the "Ark of the Covenant."

Mandy writes in her usual clear, simple style these powerful truths that will revolutionize our lives. Oh, that we all would become "God Magnets"! Let this book stretch your wineskin as you read it. The Lord has so much more for you than you can ever dream or imagine!

-**Audrey Church McIntyre**
Executive Director, House of Good Hope, Hartford House of Prayer

Mandy has been my cherished friend and prayer partner for many years, and, to me, she embodies the Holy Spirit. She carries the heart of Jesus and is pastor, counselor, and comforter to many. Her passionate and relentless pursuit of the presence of God is not only admirable, but contagious!

God Magnet overflows with a deep wisdom that has been deposited in Mandy's spirit through her intimate encounters with God in ordinary life. You will be deeply encouraged by the powerful biblical truths Mandy paints on every page with artistic imagery. Read this book and be drawn into the affectionate arms of the One who loves you the most.

-**Joellen Putnam**
Founder of Activate the Cure, USA

If you have the joy of knowing Mandy like I do, you get to read this book with the vision of her infectious smile and the sweet sound of her South African accent. *God Magnet* is a beautiful combination of heavenly perspective and personal challenges that, if followed, will change your world and the lives of those who are in it. This work is a powerful integration of life-giving teaching and the breaking off of dead religion.

Pastor Bob Switzer
Family Life Pastor, Faith Worship Center, Pepperell, MA

One of my favorite passages of Scripture is Psalm 84:3 where it says, "Even the sparrow has found a home, and the swallow a nest for herself, where she may have her young—a place near your altar." I love this passage because it describes the very nature of God's presence—everything in God's presence is productive and full of life.

God Magnet paints a vivid and compelling picture of the awesome privilege we have as God's sons and daughters to carry and release God's presence everywhere we go. Mandy warms our hearts with many relatable life stories in each chapter as she allows us little peeks into her life's journey. She challenges us to be a flexible wineskin in our mindsets, prepared and ready for the new expanding ways of the kingdom.

It is an honor to recommend this book. Mandy Adendorff is a beautiful woman of God inside and out. Her life and all that she brings with it is an amazing gift to the body of Christ.

Pastor Jerrica Watrous
Worship Pastor and Senior Leader, Friendship Church, Ledyard, CT

Some people write a book because they have academic knowledge; others, like Mandy Adendorff, write because of passion and personal experience. That makes for a powerful book that is a prerequisite for anybody who is serious about God's kingdom.

Dr. Chris de Wet, Ph.D.
Global CEO, AFMIN

God Magnet is a wonderfully accessible presentation of the good news of God's love and life for all who believe in His Son, Jesus. Written in almost a daily devotional style, Mandy invites us to grasp profound truths and power through simple and clear illustrations and teaching. The windows of understanding she shares are food for the seeking heart and the new believer. And for the mature believer, they are a refreshing drink.

Pastor Wesley Zinn
Wellspring Church, Berlin, CT

Dedication

This book is dedicated to my incredible family, who has always and at all times believed in me:

To my dad, Ian Isaacson, I will never forget the day you arrived home with a little tinsel Christmas tree. I had nagged you for one, but could never have known at five years old what a big deal it was for you, a Jewish man, to give such a thing to your daughter. You would have done anything for me, and this I knew. What a gift to have had you and Mom cheering for me all these years.

To my mom, Gilda Isaacson, your steady love, patience, and considerate heart have been a treasure to me. Like Dad, you would have done anything for your children, including changing continents to be with us.

To my husband, Stuart, where would I be without my knight in shining armor? You are that and more. You have taught me about adventure, loved me every day, and have never stopped dreaming with me.

To my gifts from heaven, Lindy-Joy and Jenna, I am in awe that my two beloved babies could become my two closest friends. My heart cannot contain the joy you bring to me.

To my sister, Tracey, I have always felt your love and faithful prayers. When God gave me a sister, He not only gave me a forever friend and fan, but a personal intercessor like Jesus.

Contents

Foreword

I magine what it would be like for God's magnetic love to lock on to your heart. You feel the fiery presence of the One you love drawing near. Your spirit comes alive with the thought of God, the living God, setting His gaze upon you. Then the realization dawns: you are His dream come true, the fullness of His desire realized. When you were born, God spoke the words over you, "My desire is toward you! You will be Mine!" How does it make you feel to know that you are God's dream come true?

The Father has invested so much in you; it's too late now for Him to pull out. He will finish this "good work" and make you complete in Christ. Sacred blood was given to save you, and sacred wind was breathed upon you and empowers you in your journey. Everything about you now reflects the Father, the Redeemer God. Your troubles take a vacation and the glory of your Father rests upon you. This is the God Magnet.

A loving father always leaves an inheritance for his children, and your heavenly Father will exceed them all. God longs to give a blessing to His children. Every good and perfect gift comes down from our Father of Lights, and He loves to shine His glory on His kids! Mandy says it well, "He is looking for a child, a lover, a friend." God's passion is to find a partner—someone with whom He can share His secrets and His wisdom. The joy of being His lover is that we get to know Him and hear the whispers of His heart.

Life can often dim the light of His desire for us. Everyone I know struggles with something. Everyone is on the journey of finding true love, true acceptance, and true destiny. So often, our difficulties hide

13

our destiny from our view, pushing us to live in shadows rather than substance. But the God Magnet locks on to our souls and brings us into the light of a new day.

This is a day of new grace given to the lovers of God. He is giving us new wisdom to find His heart and discover His ways. It is a new day full of opportunities to those who want to extend the kingdom of God. New wineskins, new wine, new mercies, and new doors are awaiting! Never in the history of the church has she been positioned to enter into kingdom glory. The Lord Himself is pulling closer with the God Magnet locked on to our souls.

You have in your hands a divine map for your journey. It is full of insights and revelation that will change your life. Mandy Adendorff has given us a GPS, a God Positional System, to realign us with God's purpose. Heaven's full access is revealed and opened for you. Step in, take your place in the flow of eternity, and find the eternal keys that unlock the heart of God. This book will bring you face to face with the God of flaming desire. This is the day of God's dreams being fulfilled. He is changing His bride from the inside out, transforming us into the radiant partner of God. *God Magnet* will show you how.

Get ready for some of the greatest changes to come into your life as the God Magnet locks on to you! You won't be able to resist this love and grace until His dream is fulfilled. He has sought for you. He has rescued you. He now is ready to partner with you as His royal friend. You are now His ark of glory on two legs. You are His dream come true! Enjoy!

Dr. Brian Simmons

Stairway Ministries, and author of *The Passion Translation*™ Project

Introduction: What's with the Wineskins?

#freefromtoxicreligion

Sacred Hearts and Sacred Kingdom

J esus spoke this riddle: "No one pours new wine into old wineskins. Otherwise, the wine will burst the skins, and both the wine and the wineskins will be ruined. No, they pour new wine into new wineskins" (Mark 2:22). All old wineskins were once new, but over time leather hardened and set into one position so that it could only contain the old wine. An old wineskin is like a heart and mind that becomes fixed into a certain system of believing; if the new wine of the kingdom is poured into this old wineskin, it will not be able to be contained in the immovable quality of the old leather.

New wine has qualities similar to that of the kingdom, which increases and expands. The old wineskin would break from the new wine because it would be unable to stretch and the new wine would spill out and be wasted. This is a tragedy because the wineskin of human hearts and the new wine of the kingdom are both sacred.

When our hearts have preconceived ideas about God because of past experiences, we may have no room for the new expanding ways of the kingdom. If God was to pour His increasing kingdom into these old wineskin hearts, the kingdom would not fit into the old, set ideas and would be rejected. The release of God's kingdom would burst the wineskins. This is not a positive breaking, but a destructive breaking that Jesus was referring to, because when we reject the work of God our ability to know, hear, and contain Him becomes broken.

God Magnet

This is why John the Baptist had such an important task—to prepare the way for Jesus. He was not preparing the literal roads and highways in the region; he was preparing people's hearts and minds—their wineskins. His ministry was to prepare people's hearts so that they would not reject Jesus. Their hearts had to become so desperate for God and His kingdom that they would be willing to turn from familiar mindsets and be ready to receive the new wine that God was about to pour out, whatever it looked like.

In those days the kingdom was about to be released in a way that looked very different from the days of Moses and the Law. This could be confusing to people, and God wanted them to be ready and able to receive what heaven was about to pour out. God always wants us to be able to receive His goodness. These people could not have imagined the manifestation of God that was about to be revealed to them, so how could they be ready to recognize and receive Him? They needed to position their hearts into a place of flexibility to receive the kingdom, no matter how it came and how different it seemed from past experiences. God sent John to prepare His precious ones for the coming wine.

But many religious leaders rejected the new wine. They rejected Jesus simply because they rejected the message of John the Baptist, refusing to prepare and change their wineskins: *"But the Pharisees and the experts in the law rejected God's purpose for themselves, because they had not been baptized by John"* (Luke 7:30). They could only receive the old because their hearts had never gone through this repentance process of fully turning toward God at the expense of old familiar ways. They were stuck in an old way of thinking, and when a new way came that challenged their ideas and experience with God, they froze and rejected it. They refused to make the hard places flexible; they had a way that they had learned and taught and invested their lives into and this was the only way that they would receive the kingdom.

The Blood Can Be Wasted

When the kingdom came, it seemed wrong and foreign to many Pharisees and experts of the Law and they became broken wineskins;

they wasted the blood that could have saved them and they became broken. They simply could not contain the new thing that God was doing. Their hearts had grown to idolize their ideas above God's and they became self-deceived. The light that they thought was light inside of them was not light at all, but darkness, and they could not discern it.

There is a story of a man born blind who was healed by Jesus. This was an amazing miracle because the man had been blind all his life. Unfortunately, instead of celebrating with this man (that would have been the natural, human response), the Pharisees were offended.

The story of the healed man in John 9 reveals the fruit of an old wineskin:

1. The old wineskin is skeptical of a work of God that does not involve it:

Jesus declares that the work that He was doing was God's work. The Pharisees did not recognize the work that God was doing in the earth because it did not come under their authority; instead they became skeptics. (See John 9:4.)

2. The old wineskin cannot rejoice in another's blessing if it's not in the realm of its experience:

The Pharisees could not feel natural joy for another person's healing, because this manifestation was not in their realm of experience. Their jealousy and envy was beginning to be revealed. (See John 9:10.)

3. Rules rule. The old wineskin knows the written Law very well, but it doesn't know the spirit of the Law:

The Pharisees determined that Jesus was not from God because He did not keep the Sabbath according to the Law. These men didn't know God's heart and nature behind the Law. They only knew the letter and concept of God, and they refused anything different from what they were used to. If they had known the spirit of the Law, they would have understood that healing is an expression of Sabbath rest and wholeness. (See John 9:16.)

17

4. **Fear has a following. The old wineskin leads by fear and intimidation:**

Instead of the healed man's parents being ridiculously happy, they were afraid. They were so bound with fear of the Pharisees that their joy was stolen. The Pharisees held an unholy power amongst God's lambs; their leadership style was controlling as they ruled minds by fear and manipulation. (See John 9:22.)

5. **Self-accusers accuse. The old wineskin is full of accusation against people and things it knows nothing of:**

The Pharisees declared that they knew Jesus was a sinner. They were so used to operating in the realm of accusation that they even accused God without knowing it. One cannot be an accuser if one is not first a victim of the Accuser (Satan); these men were so used to receiving self-accusation and giving accusation that they had their consciences seared. (See John 9:24.)

6. **Holy talk can disguise a fork:**

The old wineskin uses religious language to dress up its personal poverty and take advantage of God's lambs. The Pharisees rebuked the healed man by telling him to give glory to God and not to Jesus. (See John 9:24.)

7. **The old wineskin will use any means at its disposal to maintain power:**

The Pharisees seemed to get nowhere in their interrogation of the healed man, so as a last resort they stooped to make a personal accusation against him. They had no solid argument so they went as low as to use their religious authority to make seemingly righteous accusations. (See John 9:34.)

8. **If the old wineskin senses a loss in power, it simply discards and cuts off another:**

The Pharisees finally lost the battle and instead of humbly changing their hearts (that would be a new wineskin thing to do), they excommunicated the healed man. (See John 9:34.)

18

9. The old wineskin is rooted in hidden pride:

The sad reality is that these men probably had good intentions to serve God. Pride had seduced them to think that they were the only authorities on God, but in reality they were blind. (See John 9:41.)

This story is our teacher. The way that we prevent our wineskins from becoming old like the Pharisees is to be positioned in a continual place of repentance. That does not mean we are continually weeping for past sin. Instead we are continually in a place of being willing to change from our way of looking at things to God's way, no matter how stretching it may be.

New wineskins will ultimately become old and stiff unless they are continually stretching and being oiled and massaged by the Holy Spirit. The glory we experienced yesterday can never become a model for what we expect today. Being intentional about continually being in a humble place of flexibility with God and His children is vital. Part of the Pharisees' wineskin problem was their inability to receive God's words from anyone but their group. (See Luke 7:30.)

It's All about Change

An old wineskin heart will not only affect our spiritual lives, but other areas of life too. Proverbs 4:23 says, *"Above all else, guard your heart, for everything you do flows from it."* The condition of our wineskins influences every area of our lives, particularly the ability to deal with change. If we can't stretch with God, we will find that change in any area of life is very difficult. But when our hearts are allowed to be stretched by the Holy Spirit, our struggle with day-to-day change will get easier.

The early disciples' ministry schedules had to change at a moment's notice because the Spirit would say "no" or simply lead them elsewhere. Even though they had plans, their minds were not anchored in their own set agendas and experiences but on God, so if plans needed to change it was not such a struggle. Their anchor was God—not their address, schedules, or anything else. Their new wineskin hearts were positioned into a system of believing that flowed into their everyday lives. They were used to change from their deepest parts. It was simply a way of life for them.

Time is the tester of the wineskin. There are grandfathers and grandmothers in the church who have lived through different outpourings and change and are still current with what God is doing. They embraced the new, but were able to stretch out of that into new changes every time. Their God was always God, not a particular move, season, or style.

Being exposed to new wine does not necessarily create new wineskin hearts. A person can grow up in a new move of God and embrace the new, but still have an old wineskin heart. As soon as the wineskin must stretch to receive a different season, it can't because the new wine became God instead of God being God. This is often why revival isn't sustained and dies with the fathers and mothers of that revival. Revival can only be sustained when the revival doesn't become a form or God.

Let Your Wineskin Stretch

I Ponder:

If I am not growing in my understanding and experience of the kingdom, I am probably stuck in an old wineskin. The kingdom is so immense that if I am willing I will be continually stretching.

I Realign My Wineskin:

It is painful to change the way I think. It requires that old structures in my mind move aside to make room for the new. That can feel inconvenient and uncomfortable—breaking my neat formulas and forcing me to depend on Him alone for understanding.

I Believe:

I am willing to receive the kingdom, no matter how differently it manifests from the way I am used to or imagine it to be.

I Activate:

Expect God to reveal His kingdom to you in ways that require you to shift your mindset in order to receive the new wine. God may have moved powerfully through a particular culture or style in the past, but God was never contained in that conduit and He may want to move through a different flavor right now. If we are fixated on trying to resurrect what He did in the past, we may miss what He is doing right now. Let your wineskin stretch and take a risk.

Section 1:
God Has a Dream

We sing about it, we dream about it, and we cry out for it—*more of His presence*. This is no new concept and it didn't originate with us. This has always been God's dream. His dream of being palpably present with us can be seen throughout history—from old covenant encounters to latter day renewals—and His dream is being fulfilled right under our noses. It's best we take a closer look.

1. God's Impossible Dream

#you'reit

My First Time

The first time I encountered Jesus was in my bedroom. I was a young woman, but had never put a foot in church. I had wavered from my strong Jewish faith as a little girl and preferred the open-mindedness of being an agnostic Jew. I respected all religions, except of course narrow-minded Christianity which upset me. I reasoned that if there was a God He would be able to reveal Himself to me without the irritating arguments that I constantly got myself into. I prayed every night though, not to seek spirituality or God, but because I was so afraid. Growing up in apartheid South Africa was like living in a pot of steaming water waiting to boil over. I lived in Johannesburg, which at the time was known as the "stress capital of the world" because of the violent crime that impacted us every day and every night. At fifteen years old I had tasted fear, but I had never tasted God.

My bedtime prayers were a ritual. I couldn't find sleep unless I had asked whoever was up there to protect me. One particular evening my petition turned to tears, which was unusual for me, and from deep down inside I let out the word *Jesus*. To this day I don't know how I was able to utter that name because I was so anti-Jesus, but I did. And with it came something I had never tasted before—His sweet, thick presence surrounded me in my little bedroom. I was shocked at my prayer, but I was more shocked at the unusual feeling that came over me. I couldn't resist speaking that name through tears even though I felt unfaithful doing it. Yet the more I did it, the more I felt Him. I don't remember much more about that night except that I ended up on my carpet weeping and whispering His name.

Many of you reading this book have no doubt experienced His presence before; in fact, many people grow up familiar with His presence. That night was my first time. That night changed my life. I didn't understand the gospel at all. I didn't even have a clue why Jesus died on a cross, but that night I knew one thing for sure: Jesus was real and Jesus was good.

One moment with the presence of God changed my heart and my stubborn opinions instantly. That is a pretty potent encounter for a girl who had already decided that Jesus was not an option for her. God's presence did not leave me after that night; instead He intensified in me, and thirty years later He is still blowing my mind.

More of His Presence

This book is about discovering more of His presence. Let's start at the beginning by uncovering mysteries of His presence among the Jewish people of the old covenant.

In Old Testament times the presence of God was as good as it was terrifying. The strangest thing was that His presence rested with a mere box. This mysterious, holy box was called the ark of the covenant, and it was feared and loved all at the same time. Even twenty-first century Hollywood is intrigued with that special box! People experienced blessing because of the ark of the covenant, but people also died because of it. This was a great mystery, but as we explore His presence in the Old Testament we will uncover the unchanging heart of God and His intentions for manifesting His presence in our season.

Clue for Finding God's Dream

As a kid my favorite Jewish holiday was the one where Grandma hid the matzo for us to find. I liked the hunt as much as the prize, and I think my grandma liked it too. We humans are wired for treasure hunts. That's because God did the wiring! *"It is the glory of God to conceal a matter; to search out a matter is the glory of kings"* (Proverbs 25:2).

God has hidden lots of treasure all around us for us to find, both spiritual and natural. God likes games, He likes us to play them with Him, and He loves when we win! In the Bible He has hidden some remarkable treasure hunts, and He's waiting for us to find the prizes. The ark of the covenant was a big clue (the Bible calls it a shadow) to a very cool puzzle. With this clue we'll find out about God's dream. God has a big dream, but His dream has a problem—it's legally impossible. His dream is this—to be palpably close to people. He has dreamed to presence Himself intimately with us from the beginning, but this kind of intimacy with humanity was literally impossible for humans to experience.

So God Made a Temporary Box for His Dream

After the Israelites escaped from slavery in Egypt, God released His law to them through Moses and instructed the ark of the covenant to be crafted to contain this law and facilitate His presence.

The ark was simply a wooden box, overlaid with gold. It was made with earthly materials, but it was sacred. What made this box sacred was what it contained and what resided within it; the ark contained the Law of Moses and the presence of God rested within it. The ark was a gate, a place of access, where God could reveal Himself to people right in their physical world. It hosted God's presence permanently in the community, and the Law enabled sinful humans to coexist with His presence.

The Significance of the Law

Reading the Old Testament as a new Jewish believer was revolutionary for me, but for many years I skipped over the details of the laws; not only were they tedious to read, but they seemed meaningless and even troubling. Troubling because I couldn't figure out why the good God who I had come to know would give such strange and sometimes cruel-sounding laws. It was confusing to me too, because it seemed like the God of the Old Testament was different from the God of the New Testament.

27

God Magnet

Why So Many Strange Jots and Tittles?

The Law is home to a host of jot and tittles—minute details about the proper worship of God. When we read the detailed lists of laws we can get confused as to why God would create such difficult rules to govern a people. The Law seemed to have so many tough details that it was virtually impossible to keep. It was also very messy; the priests dealt with blood and the killing of animals all day. There was continual sacrifice for sin. Because the laws were so meticulous and revealed every sin and uncleanness, people were continually conscious of their dirtiness. If a person ate in the wrong manner, touched the wrong thing, or performed a ritual incorrectly, they were unclean.

Take heart, God never does anything but for a good purpose; He is good and has always been good. (His goodness did not first appear with Jesus; instead Jesus revealed who God always was.) Every law, no matter how strange and unusual, was significant, important, and reflected God's goodness toward people. As we uncover the mystery of the Law, we will understand new revelations about God and His presence in the new covenant.

Written in the Language of Slaves

When the Israelites came out of Egyptian slavery they had been slaves for about twenty generations. They were programmed to think and live like slaves, and even though they were no longer slaves, they still perceived life from a slave's mindset. Besides all this in the natural, they were entrenched in the slavery that they had inherited from Adam; they were born slaves to a sinful nature. The Law was first given to these people. The Law was a reflection of God's perfect heart, but it was released to slaves, in a language they could understand. It was designed to lead them into the greatest measure of freedom possible for that season of time. More freedom would come one day, but it was not yet time.

Jesus alluded to this when He reminded the Pharisees that certain laws were written because of the broken condition of people, and that it was not so in the beginning when everything was still good. Jesus revealed that the time had come when a greater law was about to be released to humanity. This new law would be the fulfillment of the written Law and the fulfillment of God's dream.

Every jot and tittle of the Law is good, even the strange ones; every law had a reason behind it. It was all good, but the Law was designed to be understood and applied by people in spiritual bondage.

Remember, God had an impossible dream. His dream was always to be deeply intimate with us. In the garden God brought the animals to Adam to see what He would name them. The naming of the animals is an example of God and man walking together and working together. God gave Adam creative ability as well. He made mankind to partner with Him.

When Adam and Eve gave their authority over to the enemy everything changed. Everything that humans were given authority over became contaminated that day—human identity, sexuality, relationship, work, earth, animals, the atmosphere, and so on. Everything became infected and began to break down on earth except for this one thing—God's love and commitment to people and His dream to be with them.

The giving of the Law was the shadow of God's dream. Even when He released the Law to a sinful people His desire was simple: *"I will put my dwelling place among you, and I will not abhor you. I will walk among you and be your God, and you will be my people. I am the Lord your God, who brought you out of Egypt so that you would no longer be slaves to the Egyptians; I broke the bars of your yoke and enabled you to walk with heads held high"* (Leviticus 26:11–13).

God gave the Law as a shadow of the heavenly reality that would later be released to earth; the coming law was prophesied about in Jeremiah: *"I will put my law in their minds and write it on their hearts. I will be their God, and they will be my people"* (Jeremiah 31:33b).

God Magnet

The Law Accomplished Three Very Important Functions

Function #1: The Law exposed the damage that the enemy's dominion was producing.

The Law laid bare the destructive power at work in the earth. We see how sin had permeated into the very DNA of people and even into the earth itself. In the Law even a little mildew was considered unclean; so was weakness and disease. Anything that was tainted with decay was considered unclean.

Decay and brokenness are the results of demonic dominion over the earth. They are the result of the bondage that covers the earth. Romans 8:20-21 describes decay as bondage. In the beginning before sin, there was no decay. Everything of the kingdom increases, but everything evil decays and diminishes.

The Law reveals that the very earth that was created to be under the dominion of God's children became corrupted—from every cell in a person's body to the environment of the earth and everything in it. Though God still owns the earth, man as a caretaker had given his authority over to the enemy, and now the earth was moving increasingly down the spiral of corruption.

The laws regarding decay and corruption seem harsh. The reality is, these laws were kind, even the ones that we cannot logically understand. Take for example the person born with disease. God was not being unkind to the person who was deformed when He said that they could not serve as a priest. The disease in their body could not exist near God's manifest presence, or the corruption that they carried would cause them to die in His Holy presence.

The Law was not created to condemn, but to protect. God has always loved people, but people and the earth were covered with darkness and decay. The Law protected people living in decay so that they could host a measure of God's presence and still live.

Function #2: The Law enabled sinful man to host a measure of God's presence.

When a candle is lit in a dark room, no matter how tiny the flame is, the darkness disappears; it is replaced by light. The darkness can't fight the light because light is more powerful; it simply ceases from existing. Light always chases darkness. That's good and bad news. Good news because God is light, but bad news because humanity is in darkness.

Sin-covered humanity would never survive in God's presence because darkness dissolves and perishes in the presence of light. A person would die in the presence of God because the sin inside could not survive the presence of God. The lifeblood sacrifice of animals covered sin and would allow a measure of God's presence to be able to dwell with man safely.

Without the continual shedding of animal blood many people would have died in the presence of God. Not even Moses could see God's face and live. Moses loved and believed God, but Moses too was a sinful man in decay, and darkness cannot survive in the presence of light. God's laws made a way for the Almighty to dwell among people and ensure that they could live and not die in His presence.

During the supreme rule of sin slavery on earth (before Christ came), the closest way God could dwell with man was in their community. His presence dwelt in the Holy of Holies—more specifically, the ark of the covenant. It was not very intimate and it was risky because people could die, but it was the best way God could commune with man. Remember, God's dream is to be with people. Though His presence was confined to a box, a tent, and later, a temple, it was only the shadow of a coming reality, the coming of God's fulfilled dream.

Function #3: The Law showed us how trapped we really are.

We are trapped not simply in sinful acts, but in a sinful nature that had permeated creation itself. The Law revealed that we need a redeemer who would not simply forgive a bad act, but recreate the nature of man. The Law revealed that everything people did was sinful—simply existing on earth was sinful. There were sacrifices required for every part of life; even the simple act of giving thanks to God needed a blood sacrifice.

Sin was not simply an intentional or unintentional act, but a nature that had invaded the genetics of mankind, a nature inherited from Adam and Eve. When they fell, their nature changed. We understand through the Law that covering sinful acts would never be enough; we needed a nature change.

Ultimately the Law enabled God to dwell with His people even in their condition of decay. Now that we understand the foundation of the Law we can move on to the exciting part—the fulfillment of His dream.

Mandy Adendorff

Let Your Wineskin Stretch

I Ponder:

Some parts of the Bible, especially the Old Testament, are difficult to compute, because the old covenant is only a partial picture, a shadow of the new. Often we see partial pictures in our own lives that can tempt us to doubt God's heart. It is impossible for God to do evil or to create evil in any form. (Even the enemy was originally created as a beautiful angel who decided to war against the God of goodness and turn the light off in himself.) God's intentions and plans toward us are always good; it is always safe to trust Him—even when our minds can't understand.

I Realign My Wineskin:

I realign my wineskin by accepting that sometimes I won't understand. God sees my life from every perspective—behind me and ahead of me; He sees what is impossible for me to see.

I Believe:

I believe God's intention toward me is always good even when my mind doesn't get it.

I Activate:

Lord, I position my heart to trust Your perfect goodness and integrity in every situation, even when I am only able to see the partial picture.

2. Attractive to God

#Godmagnet

I have a reputation of being a bit of a diva. I'm a little lady who always carries a lot of stuff. Like many ladies I learned the skill of being self-sufficient while mothering my two babies in Africa. The one item that had to come everywhere with me (beside my protein bars, water, and proper tea bags) was my toddler's sippy cup, which had magic powers. It had the power to calm a crazed child and a stressed out mom along with all the other people in our direct vicinity. The magic powers of the sippy cup kept us all happy except on those unfortunate occasions when it was forgotten. That was power, but not as good as the power of the ark.

The ark of the covenant carried real power. Wherever this ark went, the blessing went. The Law of Moses was in this sacred container, and it was placed in the Holy of Holies. On top of the ark was the mercy seat; this was where the blood for sacrifice was placed, and it was here where something remarkable happened—God made Himself known in a way that could be tangibly experienced by humans.

The ark was a gate, a type of entrance point for God's glory to be released into the earthly realm. The presence of the ark in the Israelite community was wonderful, but it was also fearful. There were times when people died because they were careless and they could not survive uncovered so close to the presence of God.

In those days His presence lived among the Israelite community, but He could never get too close to a decaying human. Though God loved people, His presence could not manifest too closely to them because evil cannot exist in the presence of God, just as darkness cannot exist where there is light. When the goodness of God comes, evil cannot breathe. That is why men died when they handled the ark of the covenant outside the protective stipulations of God. The goal of the Holy Place (whether the tent in Moses' day or the elaborate temple in Solomon's) was to provide a place where God could be with His people. Blood offerings were needed so that people could experience His presence without dying from His glory. It was the only way God could dwell in the community of His people.

But God had an impossible dream. He dreamed to not only presence Himself with people, but to be so close to people that He would actually live inside them freely with no risk of death to them. This, of course, was impossible because sinful people would die in such an intimate position to God. But God dreamed of a unique relationship that would be reserved only for God and humans, a relationship in which God Himself would make His home inside humans permanently.

In Scripture our relationship with God is compared to that of marriage, friendship, and parental relationships, but the concept of God living inside a human is unlike any human relationship possible. It is a magnificent relationship reserved only for humans and deity. Jeremiah and Ezekiel both prophesied God's dream—that God would someday engrave His law on flesh instead of stone, that people would host His living law, and that there would be no more need for a wooden box.

Beauty and the Beast

Every unbroken child believes in fairy tales. I suppose that's because we were made for them. The love story of "Beauty and the Beast" is also about an impossible dream—the marriage between Beauty and a grotesque beast who was once a prince. There was only one way for the dream to be fulfilled—the beast would have to magically transform into a prince in order to marry Beauty. In this fairytale lies a parallel to God's impossible dream.

Before Jesus ascended to heaven He told His disciples that it was better for them that He went away. Now let's be honest. How could it be better for people to be without God in skin? Could there be any greater manifestation of "God with man" than Jesus in flesh?

But Jesus was right; there was coming a greater manifestation of the presence of God than even Jesus in skin. Jesus explained before His death that the Holy Spirit had been with them but the time was coming when the Holy Spirit would live inside them—permanently.

Up until now the Holy Spirit was able to manifest Himself to people in a measure; He came upon some people at times, and there is mention that certain Old Testament folk were filled with the Holy Spirit for certain tasks, but never had the Spirit of God lived in a person in the way Jesus describes: *"And I will ask the Father, and he will give you another advocate to help you and be with you forever—the Spirit of truth. The world cannot accept him, because it neither sees him nor knows him. But you know him, for he lives with you and will be in you"* (John 14:16-17).

The Holy Spirit was about to come, and this time He would not live next to a person or rest upon a person at times. Instead He would permanently make His home inside a person. Jesus highlighted this noteworthy detail in John 14:17 because it is very important for us to understand.

After Jesus' resurrection He instructed His disciples to wait for the promised Holy Spirit. This promise of the Holy Spirit didn't originate in John 14, but was spoken of throughout the Old Testament. God indwelling man was God's long-term dream even when He first released the Law to Moses.

On the day of Pentecost the Holy Spirit was released from heaven to take up residence inside men and women—this time like a rushing wind and fire. The fire was not a single fire like the fire that came upon the Holy of Holies in the Old Testament; this time it separated into individual tongues of fire that settled on each person. God entered each person and came to live inside them. This is the baptism of fire that John the Baptist prophesied (see Matthew 3:11).

God Magnet

You would think that this encounter with the holy presence of God would have killed them, but they did not die. God had prepared His people for this moment. How had He prepared His people so that they could contain His glory without dying? Before Jesus went to the cross He said these words, *"Now is the time for judgment on this world, now the prince of this world will be driven out"* (John 12:31). He was describing what was about to happen: God's righteous judgments that had been withheld for so long were about to be unleashed on the earth. Shockingly the judgment would be focused on only one person— Jesus. Jesus Christ would stand in for the convicted crimes of every soul and receive the full judgment that would bring justice. This would result in the driving out of the prince of this world, the enemy who had usurped people's royal authority; he was driven out like darkness that disappears in the presence of light. From this time on, the kingdom would move forward freely and darkness would have to give way to light.

Jesus had to die and rise again before the Holy Spirit could enter people. *"'Whoever believes in me, as Scripture has said, rivers of living water will flow from within them.' By this he meant the Spirit, whom those who believed in him were later to receive. Up to that time the Spirit had not been given, since Jesus had not yet been glorified"* (John 7:38-39). It was only after the cross, after the victory over sin and death, and after Jesus was seated in heavenly places that man was ready to receive God's presence within. The work of Jesus was fully complete; there was nothing left to do.

Jesus had been glorified and seated in heavenly places with Father God, but He was not alone. He had purchased seats with Him so that we could sit together far above every sinful power and principality. Man and woman were changed. Human sin had been paid for, releasing perfect forgiveness to everyone who would receive it. The forgiven person received God's righteousness in place of his unrighteousness and his nature was recreated. It was just like the fairy tale of "Beauty and the Beast"—the beast had become a prince; finally he had been made perfect for Beauty.

God's Dream Fulfilled

No longer did God have to live in a community to be close to His people; now He could live *inside* His people. Humans have become the new ark of the covenant—vessels not made from dead wood and gold, but from living human dust and Jesus' glory.

Just as the first ark was a gate and an entrance for God to manifest Himself on earth, we have become the gate and access point for heaven to be revealed on the earth today. But the human vessel is not just a functional vessel for God to use; we are His beloved, His prize. Our humanity is good and attractive to God, and this new God-human relationship revealed from heaven is the fulfillment of His impossible dream.

The New Law Is a "He"

The law of the Spirit is not an exhaustive list of laws that gets engraved on our hearts; the law is no longer an "it" but "He." The living law of the Spirit that Jeremiah and Ezekiel prophesied about is a person, the Holy Spirit. *"Therefore, there is now no condemnation for those who are in Christ Jesus, because through Christ Jesus the law of the Spirit who gives life has set you free from the law of sin and death"* (Romans 8:1-2). Notice that the law of the spirit is referred to as "who," and He who lives in us is not a force or a list of commands, but God the Holy Spirit!

The new law is placed inside a sacred container—a living, breathing vessel covered not with gold but with God's righteousness, and sprinkled not with the blood of animals but with the precious blood of Christ. The old ark of the covenant was built to receive and contain the Law of Moses. The new ark of the covenant was built by Jesus to receive the fulfillment of God's dream—the new law of the Spirit.

Tablets of Human Flesh

Now our hearts have become the new tablets made of human flesh. The Holy Spirit has become the living engravings on our hearts. He lives in our hearts to comfort us and teach us everything we need to know. We are not governed by an outward letter anymore, but by something much greater—the law of the Spirit who lives inside us.

We now know the law personally. When we look to the Word, it is not because we do not know how to live; instead it is because we do know—we know what He tastes like and we hunger for more. His Word becomes our lover; we know and He reveals more. Revelation becomes our daily bread, and it is not scarce because revelation lives inside us and *"deep calls to deep"* (Psalm 42:7). The Bible is not a hard book of commands anymore, but a living Word that connects with the law inside of our new wineskins and gives birth to more revelation.

The Law of the Spirit Is a Living Person

The tablets of the Law were also called *testaments*. The laws testified and gave witness about God and His ways, but that was the shadow. Now the Holy Spirit is the new testimony of God; He testifies with our spirit, bearing witness with us on the deepest level of who God is and who we have become in Him. That is why it is impossible to persuade a believer that God does not exist, because the testimony of God is not a persuasion of the mind but a living person. That is why I, as a brand-new believer, knew that I was God's daughter simply through my encounter with Jesus as His Spirit testified to me who I was. *"The Spirit himself testifies with our spirit that we are God's children"* (Romans 8:16).

The law of the Spirit can never be learned, but *imparted* because He is a living person. We now know how to live by the Spirit who teaches us continually. This does not diminish the Bible at all; it fulfills it, because the Bible can only be interpreted by the Spirit.

The New You: New Covenant Ark

There is no longer a sacred box for God's presence to manifest upon; now we have become the beneficiaries of the fulfillment of God's dream. Man, filled with the Holy God, becomes the meeting place for God and humans, heaven and earth. You and I have become the ark of the covenant in our present age.

The living law residing in living people defines this season of time. God's attraction to humanity has never wavered, but has been woven carefully through history until we have seen His love revealed so explicitly through Jesus and His promised Holy Spirit. Now we have become the lovely dwelling place of God!

Let Your Wineskin Stretch

I Ponder:

Ponder this lie: The glory of Old Testament times is greater than our modern address. We don't experience anything close to those encounters and it is unlikely that we will ever see anything like it in our day.

Now ponder Scripture: *"Now if the ministry that brought death, which was engraved in letters on stone, came with glory, so that the Israelites could not look steadily at the face of Moses because of its glory, transitory though it was, will not the ministry of the Spirit be even more glorious? If the ministry that brought condemnation was glorious, how much more glorious is the ministry that brings righteousness! For what was glorious has no glory now in comparison with the surpassing glory. And if what was transitory came with glory, how much greater is the glory of that which lasts!"* (2 Corinthians 3:7–11).

I Realign My Wineskin:

I realign my wineskin to expect what God has made possible; my address has become His address. There has never been a greater time than now for me to begin to experience what He has dreamed for me.

I Believe:

I am a recreated, living ark of the covenant. I contain Him, the Spirit of the Law, and I attract His manifest presence. I am a magnet to God.

I Activate:

1. Look at yourself in a mirror; look past your flaws and see yourself as a sacred treasure chest where He lives.

2. Now speak truth over yourself: "[*Place your name here*] is a holy, sacred, loved child to whom God is attracted. I am loved, and I have the capacity to love like God."

"The mystery that has been kept hidden for ages and generations, but is now disclosed to the Lord's people. To them God has chosen to make known among the Gentiles the glorious riches of this mystery, which is Christ in you, the hope of glory" (Colossians 1:26-27).

3. When Heaven's Resources Become Mine

#unfairadvantage

Waving good-bye to my distraught child through the preschool window is still etched on my mind. Separation anxiety is a terrible thing for a child (and a mother). If only I could have taken part of myself and hidden inside of her, she would never have to be alone and I could tell my five year old everything she needed to know. Okay, that is a little weird and dysfunctional, but you get the point.

Imagine that we could somehow take our human spirit and literally share it with another person. I don't think science will ever come up with that one. But God did. There is a relationship that is so unique that it is reserved for God and human alone. We understand God as Father, Lover, and Friend; those are easy because we have human relationships to mirror them, but here is a new one—God as *Indweller*.

Unlike mother and child who need to eventually separate, we humans were never intended to live alone from God. Our spirits were actually created to be in union with another Spirit, God's own Spirit. He lives inside the believer, right with the human spirit, and we experience a closeness with God that is a comfort like no other. He is known as the Comforter because He does not simply come with us in life; He comes inside us and loves us where no one else is able to go. This is the fulfillment of the promise, the impossible dream of God.

If I was able to enter into my little daughter and live inside her, I would be able to share my mind and my heart with her. She would be the smartest preschooler ever and would never feel lonely or afraid. How's that for an unfair advantage? And that is ours!

The Holy Spirit lives inside us with our spirit. He reveals the mind of Christ and the deep secrets of God to us and gives us this unfair advantage as we live on earth.

Alien Mind Control?

This may sound pretty freaky, kind of like an alien invasion of our human bodies, but it is nothing like that. Believe it or not, God's not into mind control. God never takes over our mind or spirit. We will always have our own mind and our own spirit. God does not come in like a parasite to steal and take control. Of course, God could take anything He wanted and it wouldn't be stealing because He owns it all anyway, but He is meek. He withholds strength to give honor to all that He has made. Yes, He surpasses our imagination of what good is. He enters only when invited, gentle like a dove, and when we intentionally invite Him in and honor His inner presence, we are giving Him the place of honor in our lives.

If we don't give Him the place of honor in our lives, He won't usurp honor. He will simply remain where we allow Him to remain; if we allow Him to speak and act and influence us, He will. If we speak above Him and think without Him, He will not fight us. He honors relationship with us as a free gift and He waits to be freely honored and loved.

God's desire is to share close intimacy with us, not to possess us in a controlling way, but rather to inhabit us gently. The enemy tries to fake God in a twisted way by possessing a person, stealing the soul, and usurping that person's authority. God will never do such a thing. He indwells us as our sweet companion and comforter—to help us think like Him, to lead us, guide us, and be our closest lover and friend ever known to us. He has given us the unfair advantage, just as I would have liked to do for my little preschooler!

Let Your Wineskin Stretch

I Ponder:

God has never wanted to control me. If He did, He would have made me a puppet. Instead He made me a glorious being with the capacity to know Him in an intimacy untapped in any other experience of human love.

I Realign My Wineskin:

I realign my wineskin by receiving the very good news: God wants to share Himself with me. He wants to reveal His thoughts and secrets to me so that I will have an unfair advantage in life.

I Believe:

God created me to know me. I have always been His delight and I still am a magnet to Him.

I Activate:

Ask God questions. The Holy Spirit wants to reveal the heart and mind of Christ to me. Instead of trying to figure things out the normal way, I will ask Him to show me what He thinks. He doesn't only invite me to ask Him for stuff, He invites me to ask Him questions.

"And I will ask the Father, and he will give you another advocate to help you and be with you forever—the Spirit of truth. The world cannot accept him, because it neither sees him nor knows him. But you know him, for he lives with you and will be in you. I will not leave you as orphans; I will come to you. Before long, the world will not see me anymore, but you will see me" (John 14:16–19).

Section 2:

Beneficiaries of God's Dream

God dreamed it so we can live it. There is no ceiling for us who get to live out God's dream, but understanding the glory that lives within us is vital. We must see in order to seize what has already been given.

4. Recognizing Visitation

#Iamtheark

T all New England pines and other indigenous trees dwarf our home. There was a time when you could stand outside and close your eyes and not hear a sound. Not even a faint bird song could be heard. I love birds, but my birdless yard didn't bother me much until an overseas guest drew my attention to the strange phenomenon in my yard—so many trees, but not one bird.

Though my husband and I had prayed when we moved in a few years before, the Lord pressed me to prayer walk our property more intentionally. One morning I went through the property, anointing with oil, receiving words of knowledge and making declarations. (I had already known about a suicide in the home before we moved in.) When I was done I could sense a shift in the atmosphere.

The following morning I awoke at 5 a.m. to an irritating noise on the window. It was a woodpecker. The woodpecker wake-up calls continued every morning for days—no, weeks. Not only at our bedroom window, but the girls heard them at their end of the house too. I finally told my husband about this whole phenomenon and that God was healing our land, quite literally. Our conversation was interrupted. I needed to go to the garage for something, and as I opened the garage door, two birds flew out. We then started getting sneaky birds coming into our house, and our yard became home to many wonderful varieties of birdlife. To this day I still never put birdseed out because I love to see God bring the birds.

51

God Magnet

God had led me to agree with Him by bringing His authority to the property, and I have a personal hunch that birds are at home in God's presence!

Presence People

That story may sound pretty strange, but similar things have happened before. God instructed Joshua to lead the Hebrew army around the walls of Jericho for seven days for a specific purpose; the goal wasn't for an army of men to show human power by marching around a city, but for the presence of God to be taken around the city. The army was instructed to march the ark of the covenant around the city. The ark was positioned in front and the army followed; the army's job was to facilitate God's presence surrounding the city.

God could have sent His presence to pull down the walls of Jericho without any army at all, but He chose to use His people. Remember how at the start of their journey to the Promised Land God had destroyed Israel's enemies in the Red Sea? He did that without their partnership; He led His people to cross the parted waters, and when they were safely on the other side He let them simply watch the water cover Pharaoh's entire army. He was giving them a testimony and strengthening their hearts. Now God was bringing them into a greater level of partnership; He was teaching them how to move with Him, because this is His ultimate dream.

God works together with people to release His presence. That's how it was in the garden before sin entered and that's always been the plan. He chose Joshua's army to partner with Him and be the momentum to take His glory around the city. Joshua's army was aware of this. The presence of God was tangible, and they had a part to play in facilitating His presence to lead them around the city.

Moses too understood this. Whenever the ark set out, Moses said, *"'Rise up, Lord! May your enemies be scattered; may your foes flee before you.' Whenever it came to rest, he said, 'Return, Lord, to the countless thousands of Israel'"* (Numbers 10:35-36).

Joseph (with many others) was an example of being a presence carrier as well. There was no ark in Joseph's day, but his faith was able to pull in a future season. Though Joseph was mistreated, no one could resist the favor on his life. When he worked in Potiphar's house (the house of an idol-worshiping unbeliever), this ungodly house started to experience the same favor that was on Joseph's life simply because Joseph was in authority there. If the impartation was so strong in Old Testament times even before the ark dwelt with people and when people had no redemptive Jesus and no Holy Spirit inside, imagine the glory that we carry!

Recognizing Visitation

Jesus wept over Jerusalem because they did not recognize the time of their visitation. Jesus didn't weep because He felt rejected, He wept because He saw starving people walk away from a banquet. This is the time of our visitation; God has visited us by placing His glorious self inside of us. If we don't recognize our visitation, we will never experience it. We are the new ark of the covenant. We are temples of God and we carry His glory. *"Do you not know that your bodies are temples of the Holy Spirit, who is in you, whom you have received from God?"* (1 Corinthians 6:19).

Understanding Our Visitation

At age sixteen, I had a burning secret. For two years I'd kept my encounter with Jesus under wraps from my Jewish family. Little did I know that my great uncle had the same secret. It was only after his death that the family learned of his faith.

My sister and I had separate encounters with Jesus in high school, but in the beginning we were too afraid to share our secret with much of our family. Our great uncle and aunt weren't close with us, so you can imagine our shock when we heard the news that they had left an inheritance to us. We had never entertained the thought of receiving an inheritance from them, and we certainly were not the first in line.

God Magnet

At first we embraced our good fortune as manna from heaven, especially because it was during our college days, but it was critical that we went through the process of learning the legalities and details of our part of the inheritance. We needed to figure out what was legally ours and how to access it or our good fortune would remain dormant.

The impartation of God's glory inside of us is astonishing, but we must set out to understand and walk in our inheritance, because it is possible for God's dream to remain an inheritance untouched.

Let Your Wineskin Stretch

I Ponder:

Imagine God creating you as a tiny baby; He made you to be a treasure chest. No matter what has happened between your birth and now, you are still a treasure chest.

I Realign My Wineskin:

I realign my wineskin to think like God; God recognizes that I carry Him. When I can recognize this, my life will take on a new level of significance. A greater intentionality will fuel my living and dreaming.

I Believe:

God and all of heaven have my back. I am a carrier of His presence, and those who rub shoulders with me experience a taste of His presence when they do. God intends to release His kingdom through me.

I Activate:

1. The earth is yearning for the sons of God to be revealed. I must embrace the revelation of who I am and who I carry so that I can reveal Him to the earth. (See Romans 8:19.)

2. Release a declaration over yourself: *The hope of many rests in me. The kingdom of God lives within me. I am God's vessel.*

5. David's Prodigal Moment

#worththerisk

Have you ever had an experience in life where it seemed like God didn't make sense? David had one of those with the ark of the covenant. The power of God's presence exuded from the ark of the covenant, and wherever it went the people were blessed. Living in the community around the ark was like living in a God bubble.

But King David had a bad experience with the ark of the covenant as he attempted to do the right thing, but in the wrong way. He attempted to bring the ark back to the city of David after it had been taken captive by enemies. In the process of transporting the ark tragedy struck. An innocent man died as he tried to prevent the ark from falling; the man touched the ark of the covenant and immediately he died. (The story is found in 2 Samuel 6.)

The handling of the ark had specific instructions that involved specific handlers who were cleansed by blood sacrifice. Men would die in His manifest presence because darkness cannot survive light, so the ark needed to be handled correctly (by priests who had been cleansed with blood). Remember, God had given the regulations of the Law to protect sinful people from being destroyed by the light of God's presence. It was never God's desire to destroy people, even in the Old Testament. When the Law was kept, sinful people were able to live in God's presence and not be destroyed by His light.

This incident broke David's heart. He was responsible for this man's death. He must also have been dismayed and afraid. He did not know how he could ever bring the ark back. Though he loved the ark of His presence, he was afraid of the ark and what might happen if they persisted in bringing the ark home, so he made the decision to leave it at the home of an "ordinary" guy—Obed-Edom (we'll just call him Ed).

Of course Ed and his house did not remain ordinary. Ordinary cannot remain ordinary in God's presence. A while later news came to David about Ed the Ordinary—his entire house had become unusually blessed! Blessing always follows the place when the ark is honored and cared for.

When David heard of the blessing he must have burned with desire to have the ark brought home. He was driven to face his fear head-on, and instead of running from the issue he set in motion plans to bring the ark home.

I believe he must have researched the Law and discovered why the tragedy had happened, but I think he was still afraid. Yet he was so jealous for the presence of God that he took a huge risk and brought the ark back—this time doing his best to make sure all instructions for the handling of the ark were followed correctly.

Imagine the joy when the ark of the covenant finally arrived home and everyone who brought it back came in safely into the city. So overwhelmed was King David that he worshiped in complete abandonment. His conscience was clear for the first time since leaving the ark at Ed's house because now he was no longer withholding the ark from the people. Now the glory that he had held back out of fear was home!

The emotions David experienced must have been like that of a prodigal coming home—relief and joy. The ark was home in glory and safety. As a leader David had no more guilt; instead he had complete freedom. When we follow the voice of God (even at great personal risk), we move in greater freedom because we know we are walking in agreement with heaven.

The Riskiness of Leadership

David had had the power to bring the ark into the city of David before, but he had withheld this blessing from the people. Instead he led in fear. He was afraid of all the unknowns that the ark of the covenant could bring, including the possibility of another death. King David was looking out for the people from a human perspective alone. Unfortunately our well-intentioned fears often prevent us from entering into the next level, and if we lead from well-intentioned fears we prevent others from entering too.

Leaders, like David, carry the responsibility of facilitating His presence within a community even at great risk. God's presence is unpredictable and there is always a price to pay for more of Him, but if we as leaders withhold Him out of fear, we will be like David—always unsure of what could have been and looking with jealousy at those who have Him in their midst, who are experiencing blessing. That blessing is meant to provoke us so that we can no longer stand our lack and are willing to risk everything to have more of Him in our community.

Let Your Wineskin Stretch

I Ponder:

Imagine this picture: You are standing in a road. In front of you is an open truck with people standing in the back. You recognize these people; they are people of faith whom you have longed to be like. The truck is moving slowly away from you, but there is still time for you to jump in. You will have to take a risk and jump onto the moving tuck, but now is the time. You must jump in while the window is available.

I Realign My Wineskin:

I realign my wineskin by thinking like God—He wants to activate His supernatural power in my life and the lives of those around me. I am a gateway for heaven to move through. David was a gateway, and like David I will be led to take risks in order to bring His glory into my natural sphere of influence.

I Believe:

God is for me, not against me. God is looking to release His kingdom through people like me. I am a gateway between heaven and earth. I am not defined by fear that used to limit what I could and could not do. I am defined by my Father who enables me to step out into new territory.

I Activate:

1. Make a decision to intentionally stop and listen to Holy Spirit during your day.

2. When you think you hear Him, take courage and act on what you hear. (Nine times out of ten, that act will involve a risk.)

3. Prepare yourself mentally to be willing to take risks—before the opportunity comes. This is what Jesus would call counting

the cost. We do it before the opportunity arises so that we don't hesitate and miss the window when it comes.

6. Wired to Carry His Presence

#atmospherechanger

The night I arrived in Dallas there was pandemonium in the airport. My connection to Colorado was canceled as were all flights for the night. I was on my way to my daughter's graduation. Airport stress hit the place and crowds headed in all directions trying to find accommodation or some alternate way to their destination. Here I was on a God journey (because every journey is a God journey when you carry Him), and my path suddenly changed. I was disappointed, but I knew He was in control.

Then came decision-making time—which flight, which route, which hotel? Oy vey, not my specialty! It may sound ridiculous, but I froze. I watched the frenzy around me, and I just didn't know what to do. I asked God to show me what to do (that's always a great option when you're in a mind-freeze), and I felt Him say that there was no special path, that whatever I chose would become blessed because I'm an ark of the covenant, a carrier of the Holy Spirit. Whew, talk about a stress buster.

Sometimes we worry a great deal about which "earthly" path to walk in when we are already walking on the perfect path, because the decision to walk with God in obedience will ultimately cause our earthly paths to be blessed. We choose the path that we believe is the best one, and sometimes we are right and sometimes we are wrong, but God will bless wherever we walk because our hearts have made the most important decision—to walk in agreement with Him.

God Magnet

That night I had a dream in the hotel room: I dreamt I was on the flight and the Lord told me that I and another person on the flight were protecting the flight. When I awoke I understood that because the two of us were arks bringing His presence with us, the whole flight was protected and blessed. I was humbly conscious of this the next morning when I was given the last seat on a flight to my destination.

On a humorous note, while waiting on standby I was curious to see who the other ark was so I attempted to watch people discreetly. I noticed that every passenger called by the flight attendant was a pastor. I was so blessed by all the arks getting on the plane, and here I was expecting only two of us. Then I heard the flight attendant call the last passenger on the list in her foreign accent: "Pastor" Mandy Adendorff! *Passenger* sounded so much like *pastor!*

We carry Him into every place we go, and our presence can literally change the atmosphere for other people. The kingdom is like a little yeast that eventually causes all of the dough that it touches to increase. (See Luke 13:20-21 and Isaiah 9:7.) We carry the dominion of the king. We may appear normal and possibly even insignificant, but the yeast that we carry will bring increase to everything it touches.

Resting through Storms

Another evening I was flying to Texas; I was looking forward to some sleep on the plane, as I was exhausted. I had just finished a conference that day and was to minister the following morning. Shortly after take-off the pilot told us that we would have to fly through a storm, flight attendants had to remain seated for the entire flight, and refreshments could therefore not be served. My heart sank; I could survive without my tea, but the turbulence worried me. Turbulence always makes me feel sick, especially on smaller aircraft.

I intentionally took my focus off the sick feeling that fear brings by thinking of His faithfulness; I started to quietly thank God that He would clear the storm and that this would be a turbulence free flight. As I thanked Him I sat back and rested in His presence. After about fifteen minutes of very smooth flying the pilot announced that the turbulence was still coming. He warned us not to get out of our seats even though it was smooth. He made the same announcement some time later and then was silent for the rest of the flight. The entire flight was perfectly smooth; I didn't feel even one tiny bump.

God is moved by our little issues (even though some of ours may seem pretty pathetic compared to those of most people!). We get to walk in His wonderful kindness, and this kindness shown toward us overflows and extends around us wherever we go. People are blessed when we are around. Not only was I blessed on that plane, but everyone else was too. Because we have opened our lives to His presence, others around us are blessed too.

It is not presumptuous to know that His favor rests on you; nor is it presumptuous to know that the atmosphere will change where you go. You carry His presence wherever you go; it is not pride or presumption— it is the gift of God in your life. His goodness is His glory and where His goodness is seen in your life, so is His glory.

Let Your Wineskin Stretch

I Ponder:

Ponder a situation in your life where the atmosphere is void of peace—maybe a family situation, your workplace, etc.

I Realign My Wineskin:

I realign my wineskin by thinking like God. God doesn't think a toxic atmosphere is normal. I don't have to accept it as normal either, but I can be a gateway for heaven to flow into that atmosphere.

I Believe:

God is good and wants to bless the little issues of my life. God desires to show His kindness to me and to others in this situation.

I Activate:

Take authority over a negative atmosphere and allow your heart to rest in hope. By simply changing my beliefs about the situation and believing God to show up, I become a gateway for God to release His life through me into the situation.

7. When Rewind Doesn't Work

#heaven'srestorebutton

I sat in the backseat of my dad's Wolsey trying hard to hide the tears that mimicked the rain outside. I was only ten years old, but I was grappling with some deep philosophical issues. I had seen an elderly, dignified looking man walking alone with his parcels in the rain. I knew he had suffered, because it was 1979, he was black, and this was Johannesburg. From the youngest age I can remember being distressed with what I saw and heard. My heart would faint when I heard of some of the atrocities that went on around me. I could not fathom evil; it seemed so powerful and affected so many innocent people.

The world which was created to be very good had become very evil. Suffering and death entered the world through one sin. The Bible teaches us that *"sin entered the world through one man, and death through sin, and in this way death came to all people"* (Romans 5:12).

This one deed opened the way for the deluge of evil to enter our lives and world. It had to be a terrible sin, but have you ever wondered what it was? (Please tell me it had to be worse than eating the wrong food.)

Let me digress for a moment. God's character is better than we could imagine. Everything good, perfect, and wonderful originated in God's heart first. It may be difficult to imagine what God's character is like before we taste Him, but He has revealed Himself in creation so that everyone can see His heart. We can all relate to the joy of a little child, the passion between a man and a woman, the warmth of the sun, and the glory of the ocean. All these things come from God's imagination. If you love the good things in life, you will love the One who made them. He made these wonderful aspects of life for people to enjoy. Like the sprinkles on a great cake, the cake is Him. Our greatest pleasure will always come from enjoying Him, and then there are the sprinkles—every other good thing in life that He has added for our pleasure!

In the light of God's goodness and kindness to us, consider what happened at the beginning of time in the garden—Father God, in love and expectancy, gave Adam and Eve the planet to enjoy, rule over, and take increasing dominion upon. God gave instruction to Adam and Eve about a certain tree. The enemy came and suggested that God was lying. Instead of believing the voice of God and agreeing with what God had spoken to them, they chose to believe another voice and, in suspicion of God, turned their hearts away from the One who loved them. Instead of believing the true voice of their Father, they chose to believe another. They esteemed another voice more highly than God's voice and came into agreement with it.

Satanic Agreement

I don't think Adam and Eve intentionally chose to make an agreement with the enemy. But when they moved their faith from God to another they defaulted into a satanic agreement. If they had maintained their belief in God's words and integrity, they would never have been deceived. The strategy of the enemy has always been the same; it seeks to divert the heart from believing God to believing any other voice. Once the mind and heart are turned away from believing God, the person will fall into agreement with another voice.

The opening for evil on the planet was simply this: Not believing God. Adam and Eve chose to not believe God's character, integrity, and words. They doubted God's goodness and justice; they thought their own reasoning voice was truer. Sin always begins with not believing God. I submit to you that all sin, decay, and evil have the same root—not believing God.

Our Greatest Failure: Not Believing Him

Consider what "not believing God" is. It is choosing to believe the power of another instead of the true God. It is rebellion against Him.

When people failed to simply believe God at His word a tear was opened in perfection and evil flooded in. In the New Testament, Jesus reveals the root of sin when referring to the work of the Holy Spirit, "*And when He* [the Holy Spirit] *has come, He will convict the world of sin, and of righteousness, and of judgment: of sin, because they do not believe in Me*" (John 16:8-9 NKJV).

Note that Jesus does not define sin by an act, but by a position of belief. That is not to say evil works are not sins, but all evil begins as a warped position of faith.

Believing Is Our Breath

We were created to believe God; it is the core of our being. If we decide to not believe God, we will still believe something because believing is like breathing for humans. It is impossible to exist and not believe something. When Adam and Eve doubted God they were simply placing their belief on another, and when they placed their belief in something other than God, they gave away everything. That is how powerful their believing was.

The moment Adam and Eve believed the enemy, their eyes "were opened" and they saw things differently; suddenly the tree, its fruit, and the concept of independent power became exciting. Whereas before, when they believed God, they were safe. Forbidden fruit had always been present, but it had not been attractive to them. It was when they shut off their belief in God's integrity that they had the stirrings of a different appetite. Instead of believing that God had good intentions for them, Adam and Eve started to believe that maybe God wasn't so good after all—maybe He was hiding something good from them. They believed an accusation against God suggested to them by the accuser himself. The enemy took this opening in mankind and usurped human authority to use for his own evil purposes.

The root of sin is this—not believing God. Not believing God is the placing of our belief in something other than God; it is the lifting of the mind and heart to believe another voice is truer, safer, and smarter than God's.

When God Presses the Restore Button

Adam and Eve's failure to believe God gave access for evil to invade life and all they were entrusted to rule over. People failed the first time. But God gave us a second chance. Jesus came as a man, the second Adam, *"For if, by the trespass of the one man, death reigned through that one man, how much more will those who receive God's abundant provision of grace and of the gift of righteousness reign in life through the one man, Jesus Christ"* (Romans 5:17).

Our Second Chance

Have you ever asked God this question: "What works do You require from me?" You're not the only one! Jesus was asked the same question by the people and His answer was shocking. He didn't instruct them to do a great work, weep for their sin, or die a great death; He simply said this: *"The work of God is this: to believe in the one he has sent"* (John 6:29).

We have a second chance. We are believers, not workers or weepers, but believers because that's the key to the second chance. We cannot rewind time. Once an action is done, it is forever imprinted on time, but God is bigger than time. God became the restore button in Jesus; He granted a way where there was no way, a second chance for us to believe in the same arena Adam and Eve had failed in the first time around.

Jesus completed the work of redemption for every one of Adam and Eve's children; now it's up to whoever will take hold of it. For Adam and Eve's children to regain Adam and Eve's place, we have to do what Adam and Eve failed to do in the garden—simply believe God. We have a second chance to believe His integrity and heart, and believe who He has made us to be. For those who believe, there is the chance to walk in the garden with God once again—this time in an even greater capacity with God Himself living in us!

Let Your Wineskin Stretch

I Ponder:

This is the great work we are all called to do—believe Jesus. "Believe" is in the present tense. Believing is the entrance to the kingdom; from the moment we set our hearts to believe Him we enter His kingdom, but it doesn't end there—it begins there. Believing Him is not a one time, past tense experience; it is a present tense, daily experience of walking in the garden with the Father. Our believing will take us any and everywhere we need to go. It is the first key and the last key.

I Realign My Wineskin:

I realign my wineskin by understanding God's good expectation of me; He desires that I believe and trust Him as a child believes his father, as a lover believes her groom, and as a friend believes a friend. This is the birthplace for everything good in my life.

I Believe:

God is better than I could imagine; He is able to satisfy every need and desire that I have in this life. God is good and will never hide anything good from me. I joyfully choose to believe Him like a child, a lover, and a friend.

I Activate:

1. Ask Holy Spirit to identify lies that tell you that something else is safer or can satisfy you more than God. Half the battle is calling a lie a lie, because lies are empowered when they remain hidden in darkness. Turning the light on them will remove their power.

2. Now choose to believe your Father's heart toward you and spend some time simply resting in His safe covering over you.

8. Remade

Adoption is an amazing concept—a mom and dad go through great sacrifice to rescue a child and make him or her their own. The child inherits a new name and a new future. We understand that we are adopted into God's family, but there is even more for us.

In this world there are no do-overs; an adopted child can't go into his new mom's womb to be born to his new parents with their blood. But we can. Jesus promised us something greater than normal adoption. Jesus promised us supernatural adoption—that we could be born again, this time through the womb of God into the bloodline of Christ.

Jesus Wasn't Kidding about Being Born Again

So what does every newborn come out of the womb with? A family history and a heritage to which all of their ancestors contributed. Unfortunately that includes Adam and Eve's DNA. But through Jesus we get to go through the birth process all over again and are born a second time. This time we are given a new nature (the DNA of the second Adam, Jesus) and a new family name (the identity of a son or daughter). Jesus wasn't kidding when He said we could be born again. It's true! *"Therefore, if anyone is in Christ, he is a new creation; old things have passed away; behold, all things have become new"* (2 Corinthians 5:17 NKJV).

Now that we are recreated beings, we are able to host His Spirit with our spirits. If we were not recreated we could never host Him inside of us; His glory would have killed us because darkness dissolves in the presence of light.

73

God Magnet

When we receive Christ, we don't simply get past sins forgiven and remain with the same old, helpless nature. What good would that do? We'd be back in the mud in no time. It would be like going back to the system of continual sacrifice in Moses' day.

When we receive Him, our innermost beings get remade and connected intimately to God through His indwelling Spirit inside of us. It is important to realize that our minds still have all the old information and habits stored. Our emotions too have old wounds and memories. We don't lose our natural history at rebirth and we don't lose our inherited blessings, but the power of the curse dies and we are given the power of a new history beginning at the cross. We are given the power to overcome old struggles because we have a remade nature in Christ.

Promise Etched into Identity

Slavery was imbedded in the hearts and identities of the Israelites who had been in Egypt for over 400 years; they thought as slaves, dreamed as slaves, and lived as slaves.

After the ten plagues, God cut Pharaoh's control off from His people. From the moment the Egyptians drowned in the Red Sea, it was clear that the Pharaoh, their slave-master, was gone from their lives forever. Their slavery was over. The Jewish pilgrims, though they looked, talked, and thought like slaves, were clearly no longer slaves. Their slave master was gone from their lives forever. They were a free people, God's people. But to change the way they lived, dreamed, and thought would take some serious mind renewal.

The Israelites were on a journey to their land of promise; the journey was long and painful for both God and His people, but through all their struggles, the Israelites were never referred to as slaves again—not by God or man. The only slavery that remained was the slavery that had been programmed in their minds, habits, and memories (the harassment that had etched its way into their lives through generations of experience and pain). In real life though, they had no slave master, only the illusion of Pharaoh who still played on the screens of their minds.

As believers we were once in slavery too, not to Pharaoh but to a sinful nature. Sin was our pharaoh. This does not mean that we simply committed some sinful acts. No, we were actually born into slavery without choice; we were enslaved by a nature that we were powerless to overcome or change. We could control some sinful acts, but we could never change our sinful nature. Even innocent children who don't choose to break God's law default to a sinful nature.

From Sinners to Saints

Sinners are not, as we would think, certain especially bad people. Sinners are normal people with kids, dreams, gifts, and strengths; they have the capacity to love and do great things, but they are trapped in a system of slavery. We can all identify because we've all been there.

Jesus never condemned sinners; in fact, God's dream is centered on sinners. Jesus loved us when we were in our worst state, and He still loves people when they are at their worst. His mission was not simply to forgive acts of sin (like lies, cheating, and adultery) because our problem is not limited to acts of sin, but with the nature of sin that we were born with. The sinful nature corrupts everything around us and causes us to be sinful unintentionally just by *being*. During the time of the Law, people lived and breathed corruption, and they needed blood sacrifice continually because sin existed in their inner beings.

We've Believed a Lie

Through the centuries we have had some mistaken ideas "grandfathered" into the church. We have believed the lie that we are confirmed sinners until we reach heaven. We identify with that because we have heard that over and over again. It has become an acceptable saying in our circles and our songs, but it does not say that in Scripture. The Scriptures teach us that we were sinners with no capacity to change ourselves. The New Testament refers to believers as saints, children, and new creations.

Jesus came to destroy the works of the Devil; He came to cut off the power of the slave driver, making him powerless over people. Jesus not only forgave our sinful acts but recreated us, making us a new breed of people, a kingdom of new creations. He literally changed our identity and transformed us from sinners into sons with new natures to match our new identities.

When the blood of Jesus was applied to our lives, not only were our sinful acts forgiven, but the sin-master's authority over us was cast into the sea. Jesus took our sinful DNA, inherited from Adam and Eve, and nailed it to the cross in His own body. Yes, He is a hero! *Sinner* was our title and identity, but no more. That is no longer our name. We must understand the difference between who we are and who we were because only sons and daughters can access the kingdom.

Appetite Change

I have to watch what I eat. I'm one of those unfortunate ones who breathes in calories. I blame it on my 5-foot, 1-and-a-half-inch height and small frame—oh, to be six feet tall with large bones! Think of all the places for fat to hide. In my eating journey I have discovered the worst way to get slim is traditional dieting because all that does is remind me of what I can't have. Instead every week I try to shop for the most delicious healthy food I can find and get excited about everything I can create and eat. The worst thing I can do is obsess over everything I cannot have.

Being conscious of bad food doesn't help me diet, just like being conscious of sin doesn't help me sin less. I'm not suggesting we live foolishly, but sin-consciousness will only take us back to the desert with the wandering Israelites. If I, as a free person, believe that I am still in slavery to a sinful nature, I will continually be aware of my sinfulness, because I will identify myself as a sinner. Though this is a lie, I will struggle more with sinful behavior because what I believe, I will do.

As long as I am fighting an old battle that has already been won, I won't be able to see my true callings in life. The Israelites had this problem too; they saw themselves as little slave bugs, so they couldn't see their true calling as warriors. Those warriors never even got to fight with Joshua in battle to take the Promised Land because they failed to see who they were in God. Instead they died in the wilderness. We are recreated to know God and live as free saints. We do not need to live in fear and expectation of slavery any longer. As a saint I am capable of sin, but my spirit is now inclined toward God, not to sin. A saint literally has an appetite change.

The Believer's Sin

Ever wonder why we are more shaken over a believer's sin than an unbeliever's sin? All sin is painful, so why is it worse when a believer sins? Because deep down we know that believers aren't driven to sin because we are not slaves anymore. We know that believers don't have to be enslaved like they were before, but this is not to say that saints do not sin. We do not condemn our brother/sister or ourselves. We operate in repentance and forgiveness and move forward. We are walking into promise, but we do that as free people living under grace and no longer as slaves. God has provided forgiveness for us as believers during this process as we go from victory to victory. This is neither a denial of sin nor an excuse to sin, it is simply the truth that we are no longer sinners. Instead we are saints who are still capable of sin but who are journeying from glory to greater glory. A sinner cannot help being sinful because that's who they are, but *"You have been set free from sin and have become slaves to righteousness"* (Romans 6:18).

Are Jars of Clay Sinful?

Jesus, though deity, was born as a man; He did not inherit Adam's sinful nature though. Instead He inherited His own clean nature, modeling for us how life could be as a new creation. He had a choice to sin and was tempted in all things. He could have sinned, but He never did. (See Hebrews 4:15.) Though He never had a sinful nature, He still had to war against temptation (and He won). From the desert to the garden of Gethsemane, Jesus warred to do the Father's will. Though He was God, He lived as a jar of clay, yet He didn't sin.

Jesus' life is a picture of how we can live—we will still war against sin, but we are not sinners anymore. And we have a God who is faithful and just, who will forgive us every time we stumble (see 1 John 1:9). There is light and life in knowing that we are no longer slaves. There is also peace in knowing that God will be the first one to forgive us when we need it. His blood will always be enough to forgive any sin. *"But we have this treasure in jars of clay to show that this all-surpassing power is from God and not from us"* (2 Corinthians 4:7).

Live Free or Bust

Though the Israelites were no longer called slaves, they had to go through the process of learning to see themselves as free people and choosing to live as free people. Every day the Israelites were supposed to take new ground in order to get closer to their Promised Land; they did this as free people not as slaves. They were free people fighting to take the ground to take possession of their promise.

We too take possession of our souls as free people. We don't become free saints after our souls are perfected; we became free saints when we were delivered from the slave master. We are on a journey like the Israelites to gain our promise, and every day we are meant to take more land. Just as the Israelites had to grow into their new identity of a free people, so do we. We do this by believing in the new identity that God calls us to be. The Israelites had to take dominion of what God had already promised them, and so do we!

Our mission as new creations is the retrieval of what was stolen. Jesus has purchased it all back for us; it is our mission to receive what is on the banquet table of heaven for ourselves and for the world. We start by believing who He says we are—saints who are indwelt by the very law and presence of God.

Let Your Wineskin Stretch

I Ponder:

If I continue to believe that I am a sinner after I have become a believer, I will struggle to be victorious. True humility believes that God can forgive and recreate me. Satan craves for me to live in my old identity as a powerless sinner. Staying in my old identity would make me like the people under the Law who were always aware of their uncleanness day and night; they lived without the cleansing blood of Jesus Christ.

I Realign My Wineskin:

I realign my wineskin by no longer expecting a slavery lifestyle but freedom. Just like the ark was simple wood covered in gold, I am made of dust, but I have been recreated, covered with His blood, and have become a home for God's presence! I am no longer a sinner, but a saint on a journey to know more of Him!

I Believe:

I am a saint, yet I am still in progress. I am confident that He who began this good work in me will complete it (see Philippians 1:6).

I Activate:

1. Imagine your life as a deep well of water. It was a bitter well with a bitter outflow.

2. Now watch Jesus dip His broken body into your well. Suddenly the murky water is changed and becomes sparkling clean. From this clean Jesus-Spring flows clean water and you are this spring!

3. Decide to no longer embrace the false identity of "sinner" and "bitter spring."

4. Joyfully embrace your true identity of "saint," and "pure spring," in your thinking, dreaming, and believing.

9. Heaven's Magnetic Field

#feedingthenewappetite

What will always get the attention of tired, bored high school kids in a food coma after lunch? More food, of course. Food is my secret strategy when I minister to high school kids. One time I asked for a volunteer to help me do a taste experiment with a chocolate cake—that was my first mistake. After fighting off the crowds (well almost), I was able to choose a young man. His job was simple—smell the cake and look at it. After a short time we asked him to describe what was happening to him physically. He told us the obvious—his mouth was watering. He felt the "magnetic" force between his mouth and the cake! (Don't worry! I eventually rewarded the brave boy with the entire cake.)

The lesson? He didn't have to try to make himself want the cake. The attraction came naturally to him. What a no-brainer! We all laughed, yet this lesson reveals something about God's heart and ours.

God thought of the idea of taste buds, and with them He created infinite flavors, spices, textures, and more. He could have made a planet with only one kind of super food, but He didn't. He created our mouths to be able to enjoy food, and He created food to activate our enjoyment. He did this for one reason—our pleasure.

People have no problem having an appetite for food; it is natural for us because we are made to love food. And so it is in the spiritual. People are created with spiritual taste buds, and when we taste God and His infinite flavors and textures we're ruined for anything else. All people are naturally attracted to God like a magnet because our heart's taste buds are made to want Him. The "magnetic field" goes both ways. We were given a natural appetite for Him and He, of course, is attracted to us.

Baptized with Ice Cream

My first baby girl was the first grandchild on both sides of the family; she belonged to everyone! She was six months old on her first Christmas. It was a hot December day in Africa, and we sat outside cooling off with a great dessert—ice cream. Of course, Lindy-Joy couldn't have any, because I was determined not to taint her diet. But you know the end of the story—family pressure, oohs and ahhs. My eventual softening led to me giving Lindy her first bite. I will never forget her expression as she tasted the cold, sweet treat—her eyes and mouth widened, as longing turned her face to quiver for more. This is how she was baptized into being an official ice-cream-loving Adendorff!

She could never have imagined what that cold mushy stuff was like until she actually tasted it. It is impossible to adequately describe taste; taste is something that must be experienced firsthand. The Bible says, "*taste and see that the Lord is good*" (Psalm 34:8a). We all have taste buds for God, but until we taste Him we just don't know. When we taste Him, it's easy and natural to enjoy Him, and we crave more and more of Him. Just like eating is a no-brainer for people, so is spiritually feasting on God. We are created with the capacity to desire Him more than anything, and He is able to satisfy our different hunger cravings more than anything else.

The only reason people may not have an appetite for God is because the enemy has blinded their hearts: "*The god of this age has blinded the minds of unbelievers, so that they cannot see the light of the gospel that displays the glory of Christ, who is the image of God*" (2 Corinthians 4:4). It is not because they have no appetite for God, it is because we are caught in a war and the enemy knows that if people taste God, darkness will lose power over them.

We are called to be salt, to reveal God's taste to people whose ability to taste is numbed. We are called to bring back an appetite for God to our generation. When salt loses its saltiness, it loses its purpose. We are asked to taste His goodness and release His flavor. If we don't personally know His flavor, we will not be able to release His flavor secondhand, and we will lack power.

Numb Taste Buds

Religion can dull spiritual taste buds. When a generation isn't taught that they have the capacity to actively engage with God, their appetite for God will shift to another god that can fill their need for spiritual reality.

Often people turn to dark spiritual fulfillment because they have not found taste satisfaction in their exposure to Christianity. They have an appetite for spiritual reality, a craving that can only be satisfied in God. There is a lie that claims God's supernatural reality can only be experienced on the other side of the grave; until then believers must survive with rules and no supernatural interactions. Ouch! That kind of warped thinking is very destructive; it causes the blind to lead the blind and the bystanders to run.

When "Magic Mantras" Cause a Revival

The apostle Paul had some unique ways to minister to his generation. On one of his evangelism journeys he got to be part of a revival. The account is found in Acts 19. It started with Paul ministering in crazy, mind-blowing miracles. Supernatural news spreads fast, and soon the New Agers of the day took note. A group of men decided to try this new technique and used the name of Jesus as a "magic mantra" to perform an exorcism, but the demon had more power and scared the living daylights out of them. They did not personally know Jesus, so it did not work as they expected. These men learned quickly that the name of Jesus is not a mantra or a tool for power, but a person.

Paul's power wasn't found in an outside force, technique, or spiritual exercise. Paul was simply united with God. He was equipped with Jesus as the power source who lived and flowed from within him. This incident reverberated in the New Age community and many came forward to burn their magic paraphernalia and follow the living God. The result of this power contest was a powerful growth spurt for the kingdom.

People crave spiritual reality. That's a God thing. The enemy has offered them a twisted supernatural world to fill their God-given appetite, and over the centuries the church has often hidden God's supernatural world.

Before I became a believer I used intellectual arguments to fight against Christ. The truth was, I wasn't fully convinced by my own arguments, but I was a good arguer! My problem was never intellectualism; I simply used it as a tool to push against the Holy Spirit's conviction. Many people grab hold of something to push against the Holy Spirit; for some it is intellectualism, for others it may even be religion.

A Taste Encounter

Saul (who became the Paul we've just talked about) had this problem too. He used Judaism to push against God's conviction in his life. His problem was not Judaism, just as the Law was not the Pharisees' problem. They were using their chosen tool to push against the pricking of God. Conviction can be scary and for many it is easier to fight than to surrender.

It doesn't take an intellectual or religious argument to change a person's heart. Arguing is vain. Intellect and religion alone do not keep a person in unbelief; it is their blindness that keeps them fighting against God. The enemy has blinded their eyes so they cannot see and believe. A person's heart can change when they get even a tiny taste of God. It is a taste encounter that brings light. Paul was able to lead a whole New Age community to Jesus through taste, not intellectual persuasion.

Feeding the New

When my husband, Stuart, was in his twenties he had an appetite for most things a young secular man would enjoy. He was a fighter pilot with the lifestyle to go with it. He knew where he was going in life, and God was certainly not in the plan.

One evening he unintentionally went to a campus church meeting. He thought he was going to a motivational lecture. As he sat there watching people encounter God, something stirred inside him and he asked God to prove He was real to him by healing his back injury. Stuart immediately felt a wave of heat pass through his back and all the pain left. He was shaken to the core, but sat in his seat quietly. At the close of the service, he stood to receive Christ.

The next night was club night, but he longed to go back to church instead. No one told him what to desire; this new desire came from within. A new appetite had been awakened in him, so much so that he had the courage to leave every tasteless thing behind.

As we honor our new nature and feed it, our true appetite will increase, and as we feed our new nature, the old false appetite will fade. Just like our bodies long for and need food, we are recreated to long for and need Him; we are not prone to sin anymore. When we embrace the lie that expects us to always struggle with sin, we will.

As we begin to understand how much God desires us, our appetite changes. Instead of constantly fighting an appetite to sin, we find ourselves longing for more of His voice and presence. Our desires change. Temptations still come and at times bombard us, but if we feed our new nature on believing God, we will have a new appetite.

Temptations lose their grip, not because we have super power, but because we crave more of His taste. "*You, however, are not in the realm of the flesh but are in the realm of the Spirit, if indeed the Spirit of God lives in you. And if anyone does not have the Spirit of Christ, they do not belong to Christ*" (Romans 8:9).

God has given us a new nature with a kingdom appetite, but this appetite must be honored and fed with simple believing! Remember we are called believers, not sinners.

Let Your Wineskin Stretch

I Ponder:

The law of the Spirit lives in me, a recreated son/daughter. My new nature is prone toward God. My new heart longs for God. The sin that used to taste good has become bitter and tasteless to me.

I Realign My Wineskin:

I realign my wineskin by understanding how God has wired me—my entire being is wired to enjoy God. God has no bitter taste at all. There is no reason for me to hold back anything from Him. He is altogether tasty, and life (no matter how hard it is) when He is added turns to sweetness! *"O, taste and see the Lord is good"* (Psalm 34:8a NKJV).

I Believe:

Jesus has recreated me and given me a new nature, which naturally loves His taste. My old nature that was addicted to toxins is dead.

I Activate:

1. I invite you to try something that I sometimes do—enjoy a meal with Him! Let His kindness undo you as you eat some food with Him. As you enjoy the tastes, aromas, and textures, be aware of His pleasure over you.

2. Rest in the pleasure He has in your pleasure, knowing that just as your taste buds crave food, your spirit craves Him.

10. God Killed Your Slave Master

#newimprints

On a recent visit to Rwanda, it occurred to me what a promising country it had become. Yet in the midst of a better life, thousands suffer silently with tormenting memories from a genocide that happened over twenty years ago. Many of the tormented are new creations, arks of God indwelt with the Holy Spirit. Yet the memory is a powerful thing.

The Memory—Carrier of Torment or Testimony

The memory is a gift from God; it was not created to carry torment, but it often does. Our memory, even after being made new in Christ, stores all information, both good and bad.

When the Israelite ex-slaves were exiting Egypt, they had only bad memories in the banks of their minds. It was God's intention for them to believe and trust Him, but ex-slaves were not accustomed to trusting anyone. They were used to one way of life—self-preservation and fighting for survival. God understood the mind war that was ahead for these people, so He raised up a powerful competitor to live in their minds and help them think differently. He gave them testimonies.

An Arsenal of Testimonies

At the very start of their journey, God parted the Red Sea for them. Then He closed the sea on their enemies so that they had a raw visual of their tormentors drowning powerlessly. God gave them a vivid picture

87

imprinted on their minds that their slave masters, their slavery, and their old identities as slaves were permanently dead. They were free.

He also gave them fresh manna every day for years. This repetitive miracle was for a reason—to instill a habitual trust and a continual memory of God's faithfulness. But God never intended for them to stay in the desert with nothing but manna. His intent was to give them a land flowing with milk and honey where bread was plentiful (see Deuteronomy 8:9). He wanted them to live in abundance, but their hearts needed to learn trust first because they would not be able to navigate abundance with slave hearts. They would be so overwhelmed that their hearts would forget God (see Deuteronomy 8:14). Remember God's dream? His highest intention for us is to be with us. If man forgot God, even God's good gifts would be meaningless and would actually lead to their fall (see Deuteronomy 8:17). This is why God had to teach their hearts in the desert through the manna (see Deuteronomy 8:16).

God understood that 400 years of pain had been imprinted on their minds, so He released a series of astonishing miracles to imprint new, healing memories in their minds. God knows the warfare against His children often takes place in our heads, so He builds an arsenal of testimonies to raise our expectation of Him in order to shift our thinking.

Created to Be Heroes

Slaves are treated like animals; they are intimidated and trained to believe that they are powerless. That is why the Jews pictured themselves as grasshoppers and imagined that others saw them like that too.

When the Jews went to spy out the Promised Land, they recoiled back to a slave's thinking. Once again they imagined themselves as grasshoppers in the sight of others. All but two men carried this past reality into their new life. All but two were ruled by past memories and disappointments. But Joshua and Caleb believed the memories and testimonies of God instead. These testimonies lived in their memories and imprinted their new identity on their hearts; they were God's free men and warriors. I don't think Joshua and Caleb had an unusual gift or were especially brave, they simply chose to believe God. Their identity was rooted in the fact that they were their Father's precious possessions and not a possession of a pharaoh anymore.

God created twelve heroes. All of the twelve spies were given the same promises and amazing testimonies to help position them for victory. But only Joshua and Caleb inherited all that God had provided.

Those who will dare, like Joshua and Caleb, to believe God's memories above painful memories will inherit new territory and lead others into it too. It is not gifts of bravery, strength, and power that make a hero; it is simply the ability to believe God. Everyone is created and called to be a hero.

Prophetic Memories

A testimony is the memory of one of God's stories. It is our weapon against foul memories. We overcome the enemy by remembering our testimony (see Revelation 12:11). The Jews throughout the Old Testament were repeatedly called to remember the good works that God had done for them. All of the festivals and feasts were primarily for one purpose—a prophetic remembrance of a testimony so that they would continue to believe God for more and pass it on to their children. They had to use their memory to remind their own hearts and minds that God was good.

Our memory is a glorious weapon against evil and can power us forward, but if we allow ourselves to fixate over disappointing memories, we will believe them instead of God's goodness. Dwelling on negative memories is not harmless; it will shape our believing and inevitably what flows from our lives. The memories that God gives us are really prophetic testimonies, weapons against tormenting memories.

Tormenting Memories That Won't Bow

There are certain situations where negative memories are uncontrollable and very painful. Often past trauma can open doors to demonic strongholds that can cause us to react and live in darkness. Sometimes these cases need intentional help. Healing of memories and breaking strongholds takes loving prayer and ministry. God has given us the body of believers for our healing; trying to heal apart from people is lonely, slow, and not God's best plan for us. Investing in healing is possibly the most important investment we can make for ourselves and our families.

Let Your Wineskin Stretch

I Ponder:

Being intentional about what memories we allow our minds to feed on is vital. We can position our believing to see good memories as testimonies and dark memories from heaven's victorious perspective.

I Realign My Wineskin:

I realign my wineskin by recognizing that the way I think is not a minor part of my life. "*As he* [a man] *thinks in his heart, so is he*" (Proverbs 23:7 NKJV). Self-control begins in my thinking. God has not given me a spirit of fear but a sound mind. I can step into having a sound mind by simply saying "yes" and "no" to my thinking habits.

I Believe:

I define my life by the stories God has given me that stir me to hope, not by my disappointing stories.

I Activate:

1. By shifting your focus. Intentionally allow your good memories to take up space in your thinking, particularly when your mind may be less active like while traveling or resting.

2. When you discern toxic thinking, simply shut it out by intentionally replacing it with good memories, God's stories, and promises to you. Shift your focus from intimidating memories to God's heart and the ways He has blessed you in the past and present.

3. Heirloom idea: Create a memory journal that records the testimonies of God in your life, family, or church.

11. The Love Secret

#conception

Colorado, 2003. I will never forget that night. I woke up with a shudder and looked at the clock. It was past midnight. I could still feel Him in the room. Some dreams are encounters, and this was one of them. God had taken me somewhere, a place I had long forgotten. It was too dark to see much, but I could understand exactly what was happening. I watched myself being conceived and created by God. I had no shape or form, but God was there in that silent, special place. He was so focused on me that I could sense His overpowering excitement. He was doing something that thrilled Him. The atmosphere was charged with an electrical feeling of heightened expectancy; it seemed like every heavenly being held their breath and waited.

The effects of my conception encounter were palpable and lingered with me for days. I had known God's love intimately, but this was so raw. I could sense stress and anxiety lose its grip over me as I sensed His ownership and love for me in a new way. There were many things to worry about, but these dissolved in the presence of my new reality. The strangest thing happened to me that night; I felt like I was his favorite, like He loved me in a way that only I knew.

The following day I ran into the bank before going to a weekly prayer meeting. I hated going to the bank. Finances were worrisome and going to the bank reminded me of that. But that day all I could think about was my encounter. As I stood in line I noticed that everyone in the bank seemed rather unfriendly. *Perhaps they too had financial burdens?* Except the lady who stood in front of me; she exuded something special. As we chatted, I wondered if she too had encountered God.

God Magnet

At the prayer meeting a woman came to sit next to me, and to my surprise it was the lovely lady from the bank. I was so excited to see her that I whispered to her as the prayer started, "What is your name?"

She replied, "Conception." I was amazed and wanted to tell her my dream, but I closed my eyes to pray as the meeting had started. When I opened my eyes, Conception was gone. I never saw her again.

God's Love Chambers

Though the awe of my encounter stayed with me for a few days, I was perplexed by something that didn't fit my theology: I truly felt like I was His favorite—like He loved Mandy in a way that no one else could know. I was embarrassed to feel like this and had never heard anyone ever admit such a presumptuous thought before. Until I realized that it was indeed true. I was God's favorite! Along with every other person He had created.

I realize that sounds illogical and contradictory, but God has revealed this mystery to us through our own lives—He has created us fathers and mothers like Him so that we can understand how His love works. When my first baby, Lindy-Joy, was born I knew I could never love another child like this. Then came Jenna; suddenly my heart instantly had a new chamber. I loved Jenna with a Jenna-love, so intimate that only Jenna and myself could share it. Jenna was my favorite and so was Lindy, whom I loved with a Lindy-love that no one but the two of us could know.

We develop new love chambers as we birth new children no matter how many kids we have. If one child is lost, we could never fill our empty chamber with another child because the original child is irreplaceable. So it is with our Father. You are His favorite. You are irreplaceable. He is intensely in love with you, whether you feel it or not.

How to Awaken Love

Knowing we are God's beloved favorites is the foundation of our faith. It is the reason He came for us. Many struggle with receiving His love. There is a secret to awakening our hearts to God's love, but it is different from the way we would expect and the way religion teaches.

Have you ever tried really hard to love God, to the point where you were frustrated, discouraged, and wondering if you're just not as spiritual as others? No one ever loved God by trying hard, just as no one ever fell in love by trying hard. Genuine love is always a response, not a work.

There was a woman who was known for her awakened love for Jesus. She's the one who anointed Jesus with perfume. Jesus tells us her secret: *"Therefore, I tell you, her many sins have been forgiven—as her great love has shown. But whoever has been forgiven little loves little"* (Luke 7:47). Her love was simply a natural response to a greater love. When she realized that she was so deeply loved, her natural response was overwhelming love in return. The other people in the room were all religious people. They were trying their best to love God, but she got it right by simply letting God love her! If we try hard to love God, we will only frustrate and discourage ourselves because love cannot be self-created. We can't make ourselves love God. Striving to create love only makes the heart harder. Our love is priceless to God, but we can never repay Him for His love and He never asks us to. His love is a gift; the expense was His.

Believe it or not, the Christian life has a lot more to do with receiving than giving. When we focus on receiving His love, we will naturally flow in great love, not to get God to love us, but because a loved being naturally overflows in love.

We aren't supposed to love on command. The commands were written for those who didn't contain the living law; but for those who do, we flow in Gods laws and ways because that's who we have become. We contain the living law, the Holy Spirit, who reveals that we are beloved children of our Father. That is the new law.

The greatest, most extraordinary miracles and works done by the church were done in response to love, not in response to law. The world needs another extraordinary work from heaven. Religion will choke the world, but people who know who is inside them, who know how dearly they are loved, will walk in the supernatural grace to water the world.

The Love Furnace of Healing

I experienced a wonderful physical healing recently. I was not in church, and I had no one with me; I was simply enjoying painting in my studio. I was struggling with fear related to a health concern, and as I painted I became acutely aware of how much the Lord desired me to trust His love and not my fear. I felt so much of His love that my fear vanished. I also felt heat go through my body, an unusual feeling for me. I knew something had happened.

A few weeks later it was discovered that the growth in my uterus had unusually and strangely vanished! I knew it had dissolved in the moment when I felt His warm love come over my body. His love is the very furnace of all healing!

Let Your Wineskin Stretch

I Ponder:

The only way to awaken my heart is to first receive God's perfect love. I am created to be loved by God. My heart intuitively knows how to love God; human love is the natural reaction to God's love just as a fish's natural reaction to water is to swim. My love can only be activated by God loving me first. When I struggle to receive His love, I will struggle to love Him. I am not the initiator of love, God is, and He always loves me first. "*We love because he first loved us*" (1 John 4:19).

I Realign My Wineskin:

I realign my wineskin by staying focused on God's perfect love for me and not on my lack of love. I rest from my struggle to perform for God's love.

I Believe:

I believe that I do not have to work for love. "*But God demonstrates his own love for us in this: While we were still sinners, Christ died for us*" (Romans 5:8).

I Activate

1. Activate your heart by simply allowing God to love you and believing how much He desires you. Take some time to just *be* in His presence. (You will be amazed how powerful your life will become as you focus more on receiving His love and less on your performance or on creating love.)

2. Intentionally take moments throughout your day to remember that He's watching you and loving you.

"*I pray that you, being rooted and established in love, may have power, together with all the Lord's holy people, to grasp how wide and long and high and deep is the love of Christ, and to know this love that surpasses knowledge—that you may be filled to the measure of all the fullness of God"* (Ephesians 3:17–19).

Section 3:

Trustees of God's Dream

A beneficiary is a privileged person who inherits a gift, but the gift does not come alone; it comes with the trust to advance into new territory.

12. Perfection Is Not the Goal—Life Is

#nomoreperformance

God likes to speak to us through dreams. There's a message right in that statement. God can communicate very clearly to us when we are in our highest state of non-performance!

Once I dreamed about a special cake. It was a child's birthday cake, like the character cakes that I used to make for my girls' birthday parties. Except this cake wasn't perfect like my cakes; it looked like it had been frosted by children. The cake was made to look like a house and on the entrance was frosted a big sloppy smile.

I was so unimpressed with the shoddy cake that I took another cake and frosted it myself. My cake turned out perfect; I even iced impeccable little pine trees all around the house. I looked at both cakes together and instead of satisfaction, I was shocked—the messy cake was better than mine. Though the children's cake was far from perfect, it felt like it was living and full of joy, but my cake, though perfect, was like dead plastic. Then I heard these words: "*Let the children build the house.*" God was teaching me how He was building His church, and it was quite different from my tendency toward perfection.

What was Jesus thinking when He commissioned a group of imperfect kids to bring His kingdom to earth? Ever wonder why He did it? He could have done a much better job. It's kind of like letting your kids "help" with your project.

God is more concerned with us than with the cake He gives us to frost. He is the greatest people-releaser of all. Think of all the imperfect people He released, from Peter to you and me—surely He had to know we would make messes along the way. He also knew that the goal was never perfection. It was life!

God releases us so that we can release His life into the earth. He knows we won't do it perfectly, but He is not looking for perfection. He is looking for an increase in life. If we think God is looking for perfection, we will hide ourselves, along with our dreams and our gifts. We'll not move until God "does it for us" or sends us a sign so that we can begin to live our purpose. If you find yourself praying and waiting for God to show you something more than you are living, you may be hiding in the fear that you'll do it wrong and get into trouble or fail.

It is when we start moving into the things we think God wants us to do that we'll begin to discover His will and destiny for us. God is not asking you to second guess everything you do like a worried slave or a fanatical perfectionist; He's asking you to pursue Him with the confidence of a son or daughter.

God always releases you to push the envelope of life and try new things. You may not accomplish everything as perfectly as you would like and you'll fail many times, but the goal is never perfection— it is life. You were created to release life into the earth, not a perfect performance. God establishes us in His secure love so that we can live and move and even fail. And even in our greatest failure, we simply fall back into Him; knowledge like this gives us the confidence to dance fearlessly with Him.

The Dancer with the "Thing"

My daughter is a dancer and after attending many a recital, I learned a thing or two about dancing. At every recital there was always a dancer who had that special "thing." The coveted "thing" caused her to capture every eye and heart for the entire show. The truth was, this dancer was often not the most highly skilled in the group; she just happened to have that "thing." It didn't take me long to realize what that thing was. It was simply an irresistible joy for the dance that had captivated her. She was too enthralled to be fearful and too delighted to allow the need to be perfect to steal her moment. She was always contrasted by others who tried so hard to perform that it was often painful to watch them. Life is a dance, and we either let go of the need to be perfect and enjoy the dance or we spend every precious moment trying hard to grasp perfection.

Giving God a Voice

Can you imagine Moses or David criticizing the ark of the covenant? After all, it was just a man-made box. They would never have done this because the box that contained the sacred was holy too! Obviously we would never criticize or destroy the ark of the covenant either, but we criticize ourselves. Criticizing ourselves is a self-destructive habit. You are the temple of the Holy Spirit. Honoring Him in the unfinished you and other unfinished believers is agreeing with God's truth. We must not forget to honor the image of God in unbelievers too, as this is a key to releasing His kingdom to them.

Remember, we have made Him our home and we have become home to Him. If we hide ourselves and our gifts for fear of others seeing our imperfections, we hide Him. (See Matthew 5:15–17.) And if He is hidden, He cannot shine through us. We give Him a voice by living life fearlessly like a child, by walking freely in our own unique way. This will cause His glory to come and we will see flowers grow where we tread. Remember, we're arks, and great things happen where we go. It's not our perfection or our performance; it's our God who lives within that does this.

When we live in freedom and throw ourselves into this wonderful life, we give Him expression. When we hide in the timidity of failure, we shut Him inside. If a child is too afraid to walk for fear of falling, he will never learn to walk. He has to be prepared to fall and get hurt in order to walk and run. Daddy God holds out His hands to us as we attempt to walk. He knows that we will stumble at times and He is prepared for that. His goal is to see us run. It is better to run between stumbles than to sit and never fall. One of our greatest hindrances in life is the need to be perfect. But perfection is not the goal—life is.

Let Your Wineskin Stretch

I Ponder:

Released people release people. When we purposefully view the people in our lives from God's perspective—that they are able to do great and impossible things—we subconsciously give them that God-message. We give them permission to try and even fail. A strange thing happens when we release others—we get released more and more!

I Realign My Wineskin:

I realign my wineskin by seeing like God sees. I am called to bring life and do *particular* things, not control life and do *all* things. God has provided others to bring life alongside me, and together the picture is perfect and complete. One person doing all the right things cannot bring completion or real life. Completion of God's will comes through all of us as a group doing His will.

I Believe:

I am a releaser of people, not a controller of people. I can empower and release people.

I Activate:

Ask Holy Spirit to show you someone in your sphere of influence whom you can empower by giving them the freedom to fail and the grace to try new things.

13. Heaven Entrusts Her Pearls

#riskytrust

I love the true story about a recovering homeless man and the couple who believed in him. *Same Kind of Different as Me: A Modern-Day Slave, an International Art Dealer, and the Unlikely Woman Who Bound Them Together*[1] tells how Ron, an affluent art dealer, trusts a homeless man to deliver his brand-new truck across the country. He trusts his new friend, Denver, or at least the best part of him does. Ron so badly wants to fully trust Denver that he allows himself to risk the possible loss of his new truck. The story ends happily as we see Denver faithfully living his new life of trusting and being trusted.

What a beautiful picture of heaven's culture operating on earth. Jesus gives us a picture of heaven's culture: "*I will do whatever you ask in my name, so that the Father may be glorified in the Son. You may ask me for anything in my name, and I will do it. If you love me, keep my commands. And I will ask the Father, and he will give you another advocate to help you and be with you forever—the Spirit of truth*" (John 14:13–16).

Jesus shows us how heaven's culture works. Look what Jesus does in John 14. First, Jesus invites us to ask Him for anything, and He assures us that He will do it. Second, Jesus says He will ask us to do things, and

---

1. Ron Hall, Denver Moore, and Lynn Vincent, *Same Kind of Different as Me: A Modern-Day Slave, an International Art Dealer, and the Unlikely Woman Who Bound Them Together* (Nashville, Tennessee: Thomas Nelson, 2006). Used by permission.

because we love Him we will do them. Then He goes on to say that He will ask the Father to give us the Holy Spirit, and there is the absolute assumption that the Father will do it.

Eavesdropping on God

Jesus invites us to be a fly on the wall and take a peek at the relationship of perfect trust within the Godhead. The relationship between Father, Son, and Holy Spirit is perfect—perfect trust based on perfect love. But Jesus doesn't show us this relationship from a distance to help us to aspire to it. He doesn't want us to remain a fly on the wall, so He invites us into it.

Jesus starts by being vulnerable and offering to be the "first to go," so He invites us to ask Him anything based on this love-trust relationship. Crazy as it seems, He offers to trust us. He is willing to trust us, knowing that we may fail; He realizes that we need His trust, because His trust empowers us to walk in this heavenly way of life.

Heaven's trust is based on love, the understanding that each one wants what is good for each other and all requests that are made are good for each one. Jesus reveals His heart to those He trusts. He gives us His pearls because He believes we can honor what is precious. He doesn't expect something from us that we are unable to do. He calls us up to take part in this incredible love and trust relationship within the Godhead. He goes on to say, *"I am in my Father, and you are in me, and I am in you"* (John 14:20b).

The love-trust relationship is not meant to be contained within the Godhead. It begins here, but is intended to flow out into our earthly relationships, bringing the culture of heaven to the place where we live—our address. *"The one who loves me will be loved by my Father, and I too will love them and show myself to them"* (John 14:21).

When Heaven Trusts Human

God is not a stranger to making Himself vulnerable. In order to fulfill His dream, God had to make Himself vulnerable to man and the enemy. Before Jesus' crucifixion He explained that "now" was the time for judgment to come into the world and that the prince of the world would be driven out. (See John 12:31.) Judgment for the world came just as Jesus predicted, but the full measure of judgment allotted for evil didn't come on the planet like it did in the days of Noah; instead the full measure was focused on one man alone—Jesus Christ. Satan was given access to carry out this judgment, and all the fury of the enemy was released against God's Son. The concept of God making Himself vulnerable to His enemy for our sake is beyond our comprehension; it is the priceless work of God. After Jesus had completed His work, He handed this priceless work over to mere people to continue to release. God has entrusted us with the work of His hands.

Jesus explained how He would equip us to continue this work—the Holy Spirit would take all things that belong to the Father and make them known to us. *"He will glorify Me, for He will take of what is Mine and declare it to you. All things that the Father has are Mine. Therefore I said that He will take of Mine and declare it to you"* (John 16:14-15 NKJV). God has trusted us with a work that is impossible through humans alone. It is only possible through humans and Holy Spirit working together.

Understanding that we are wired to carry the pearls of heaven will alter the way we live life. It will cause us to believe God for more of the hidden treasure that He longs to release to us. God's children are recreated holy, which is why He is able to release His pearls to us. Pearls are never released to swine (unholy and unclean animals), but only to those made holy by His sacrifice. He trusts you if you will receive His trust.

Let Your Wineskin Stretch

I Ponder:

Jesus left twelve imperfect people on a barren, hostile earth with an outrageously vast mandate—to continue what God Himself had begun. The work that God had begun was not just a side job of heaven, but required the ultimate sacrifice from God and heaven. Now God gives us His pearls and all of heaven is filled with hopeful expectation.

I Realign My Wineskin:

I realign my wineskin by expecting like God. He believes I can fulfill the mandate and call on my life. He is aware of my imperfections and my often-hostile environment, but He knows that all things are possible to me, His ark.

I Believe:

I am entrusted with heaven's pearls, but I am not alone; Holy Spirit lives in me, empowering me to live and dream the dreams in God's heart.

I Activate:

God called me and trusted me before I ever did anything to merit this trust. He literally gave me the pearls of heaven when my heart first whispered His name. Offering trust is risky business, but it is at the core of the kingdom. If I want to see His kingdom come, I must be willing to receive His trust which will empower me to extend it to those who need it.

14. Catching Heaven's Windows

#honoringheaven'spearls

My little Lindy-Joy was anxious for her first sleepover. We sat on her bed and contemplated Psalm 91. *"He will cover you with his feathers, and under his wings you will find refuge"* (Psalm 91:4a). We thanked God for His feathers over her life and her joy returned. In her excitement she slapped her pillow, and a single feather floated down and landed on top of her hand. The rest is history and many years later she still has that feather stuck in her children's Bible as a reminder of how God spoke to her that night. Thinking back I don't think we ever owned any feather pillows.

Hearing God speak to us personally is the most exhilarating experience in life, but it's not meant for special occasions! God speaks constantly. His voice is not reserved for certain saints and seasons. Hearing God speak is meant to be normal for all of us.

Jesus told a parable about giving pearls to pigs to teach us the concept of protecting and honoring treasure by being careful how we steward it. (See Matthew 7:6.) To me the greatest treasure is hearing God speak to me. Little Lindy-Joy learned in her moment of anxiety that heaven's pearl was all she needed—one feather, one whisper. We honor heaven's pearls by protecting and taking to heart what we think He is saying to us. This is the simple starting place for all of us. The Holy Spirit is our indwelling teacher. He has a voice and He speaks to every believer. Often we hear something inside that may be Him, but we are not sure.

That is normal. It is like an infant listening to a family conversation. In the beginning, all she hears are different sounds—voices, laughing, and whispering. These are all just noises, but as she grows she will learn how to discern who owns the voices and exactly what they mean.

"Missing Its" Are as Important as "Spot-ons"

I was driving home after an intense morning of ministry; I was tired and couldn't wait to get home. At the light I recognized a woman who worked at the local grocery store. It was a sweltering day, and she was walking home loaded with parcels. The traffic light changed and I had to go, but I felt a voice telling me to turn around and give her a ride. In my tiredness I fought the voice, but I did turn around and go back, which took a while in the traffic. By the time I was back on the right road, she was gone. I drove around looking for her to no avail.

I was bummed out that I had wasted my time and "missed" God's voice. Discouragement can come when we miss it, but our "miss its" are just as important as our "spot-on" times. These experiences are the opportunities we get to honor His voice so much that we risk missing it at our own expense for the chance of hearing Him.

I call these windows. If we train ourselves to get used to catching these fleeting windows that God gives, we will learn to sharpen our listening skills. But we only sharpen our discernment by being willing to risk missing it. If we love His voice, we will honor even the slightest whisper that we think might be Him. As we are faithful and well exercised in honoring these whispers, He will entrust us with greater words that carry greater levels of responsibility.

When we hear a voice that we think is Him we do the "pulse test"—does it flow with God's heart and the fruit of Holy Spirit? Then we step into it, even if we are still not sure if it is Him. If we are wrong it serves as a building block; without these building blocks we will never learn how to step into what we hear. We learn to hear His voice by acting on what we think are His whispers. When we honor heaven's little pearls, we will be entrusted with even greater treasure.

Let Your Wineskin Stretch

I Ponder:

Two misconceptions about God's voice:

Misconception 1: *God speaks clearly to some but not to others.* The Holy Spirit is the teacher of every believer. *"But the Advocate, the Holy Spirit, whom the Father will send in my name, will teach you all things and will remind you of everything I have said to you"* (John 14:26). God's voice is always speaking. We just don't always know how to hear.

Misconception 2: *God only speaks in certain ways.* We often put God in a box (the nighttime dream box, the vision box, the prophetic word box, the hit-me-over the-head-box, and on and on). We unintentionally close our spiritual ears because we look desperately to duplicate someone else's experience instead of looking desperately for God's heart. The truth is that we each have our own spiritual language and God knows how to speak to us in very personal, unique ways. He speaks in myriads of different ways; get ready for Him to speak to you in crazy, creative ways that have not even entered your mind!

I Realign My Wineskin:

I realign my wineskin by taking seriously the "God-whispers" in my life, those things that I think may be God's voice but I'm not sure of. When I think I'm hearing God. I will respond by taking notice of His voice. By treasuring these small God-whispers, I will be making room for His voice to increase in me. This way I will learn what His voice sounds like, and my hearing will be sharpened.

I Believe:

God does speak to me even when my past experience tells me He doesn't. I choose to believe God above my personal doubt and broken experiences.

God Magnet

I Activate:

1. Honor what He says by recording it. Write down or find some way to remember and try to record God's voice as much as you can. We're pretty good about keeping records of important stuff; we keep special letters, record history, photos, etc. You'll find that when you place great importance on His voice, you'll hear His voice more and more. For example, if you're a dreamer (or want to be), have a pen and paper next to your bed and be prepared to wake up and write the dream down before you forget it. I try to have a notebook with me at all times, even in my car.

2. Honor what He says by stepping into it. It's better to be obedient to what you think is God's word than be too scared to take a risk and never step out into what God has for you. (There is space to make mistakes in life, and if we're going to learn how to run with God, we will surely scrape our knees along the way.)

3. Honor what He says above your reputation. It's better to be seen as a fool than to miss out on riches from heaven.

15. Crumbs from Heaven

#livingonsupernaturalbread

In the book, *This Voice in My Heart,*[2] Gilbert Tuhabonye shares how he survived the Burundi genocide in 1993. Gilbert was a senior in high school when he and his classmates were taken to be tortured and murdered. In the most terrifying trauma of his life, Gilbert shares how he heard God's voice speak to his heart while he was lying under dying bodies in a fire. The words were simple, yet they gave Gilbert the courage to survive. So significant was this encounter with God that Gilbert titled his book after the experience

Gilbert didn't hear a long message from God and it was not accompanied by any physical sign. He simply heard God's quiet voice speak to his heart in the hour of death. When there was death all around him, these simple words carried the life of heaven to Gilbert's heart. Gilbert had attempted suicide in an effort to avoid an imminently terrifying and painful death, but the voice of God stirred up hope and courage in Gilbert to do the unthinkable—escape from a building surrounded by armed, crazed killers. Gilbert survived to tell his amazing story.

We may never experience what Gilbert did, but many trials carry the stench of death. Some of our trials are so deep that not even our best friends can help us. This is an instance when the help of man really is vain, when even kind actions and words cannot penetrate a traumatized

---

2. Gilbert Tuhabonye and Gary Brozek, *This Voice in My Heart: A Genocide Survivor's Story of Escape, Faith, & Forgiveness* (New York: HarperCollins, 2006). Used by permission.

heart. There is only one thing that can sustain us during these trials. It is the voice of God in our hearts. There is nothing more comforting to the distressed heart than to hear God speak.

During the exodus when the Jews traveled through the desert, they couldn't survive on natural food because the desert was too harsh. They had to eat supernatural manna from heaven. It was the only way they could survive the desert. Every day the thing that was foremost on their minds was manna from heaven; they waited and looked for the manna.

God knows how to sustain us through the desert. He knows that in the darkest hours of our lives, we cannot survive on help from the natural realm; we need His voice. Often in our trials we run around trying to find encouragement in vain places when what we really need is God's word to sustain and feed us. We need to seek God's voice like the Jews looked for manna.

Interestingly the Jews didn't have to hunt for it; the manna was always there because God is faithful. All they had to do was go out and get it. They believed that it would be there every day just as God had promised.

There is manna waiting for us no matter how dark it is. This manna has the power to sustain us and lift our spirits in any trial. If the Israelites didn't go out and collect the manna, they could not eat it. They had to get up, go out with their containers, and collect it.

Sometimes we don't think God will speak to us, especially when our hearts are discouraged, so we remain inside our tents (mindsets) of *it's impossible*. If we leave our tents for a moment and take our empty vessels in expectancy to get His manna from heaven, we won't be disappointed.

Even a crumb from heaven can feed us. The message God spoke to Gilbert was short and simple. It was like a crumb; yet that's all Gilbert needed. If God has given you a small word, don't despise it. Hold on to it and believe it; it will be enough for now. And keep looking for more! It will increase like everything that comes from heaven.

In the same way that God speaks to you, He will give you His words for others. Sometimes people ask me if I have a word for them; other times I have compassion for someone and I want to release a word from heaven to them. Many of these times I have nothing to give and could just leave it at that, but God doesn't want to withhold bread from people. I have learned that if I ask Him and take a few moments to rest and listen to Him, He always releases a word. Often it may seem like a small insignificant word, but if we will honor the little whisper of a crumb from heaven and release it to others, it will become a loaf of bread for them to eat.

Let Your Wineskin Stretch

I Ponder:

The baby in the crib recognizes his mother's voice; it is always loving and warm. As the baby grows, he will learn to discern more and more what Mom is saying to the point where the conversation will mature into an increasing dialogue between mother and child.

I Realign My Wineskin:

I realign my wineskin by receiving that God does speak to me. I have a unique language with God. I can hear Him speak though dreams, nature, words, numbers, my natural senses, etc. God can speak through anything at all. I can hear Him in an increasing measure to the point where His voice becomes natural and normal. He lives in me and I in Him; this is the way I was created to live!

I Believe:

God likes to speak to me and trust me with His treasure, and I am able to hear Him and be trustworthy. My spirit knows how to recognize His Spirit speaking to me.

I Activate:

(You can do this exercise right now with no preparation, because God likes to speak to you everywhere—not just in church or prayer.)

1. Relax in His presence—He wants to speak to you. No need to exert your own energy; it is He who speaks. We simply are the receivers. (Ever notice how easily we can hear Him in the shower or at rest?)

2. Ask Holy Spirit to show you a picture or give you a word. No need to wait for something that seems spiritual, simply take what He gives you in faith. It is often the first thing that comes to you.

3. Now take that word or picture or smell or whatever you sense, and begin to ponder it with Him.

Hint: You can use this exercise when praying over others too. Don't strive or put yourself under pressure; lean heavily on Him by relaxing and resting in Him. No need to perform or try hard in any way. Hearing God takes no sweat or effort, but stepping into action does involve faith and risk.

16. Playing Catch with God

#contagiouspeople

Ever daydreamed in church? As the preacher ministers you start hearing God speak to you, but it's a different message from the preacher's? Instead of getting mad at yourself, listen. You are simply catching the fire of revelation.

There are certain preachers whom I love to listen to, because I catch something from them simply by being under their anointing; they are literally contagious! The gift that flows from them is so strong that I receive new personal revelation when I hear them speak. The revelation I receive is not always linked to the content of their message; it often has nothing to do with what they are saying, but everything to do with the Spirit and anointing that they carry.

The Games of God

My relationship with Jennifer started out as prayer partners for a mission trip, but something special began happening. I noticed that when we just hung out and did stuff like shop and eat together, we would hear God's voice in the coolest ways. We could hear God in clearer ways simply by being together.

Jennifer and I actually caught something from being in each other's presence. God started playing games with us and it was literally like the game, Catch—He would throw something out, one of us would catch it and throw it to the other and so it went. Words and crazy confirmations started flying between us; the games became more hilarious and powerful all at the same time. We experienced an

119

exponential increase in our experience with God simply by spending time together. We started to understand that if one person could chase a thousand, then two would not chase two thousand but ten thousand. (See Deuteronomy 32:30.)

We catch each other's stuff! We hold keys for each other and we unlock each other's doors. As we unlock another's door with our key, our door opens too. This is why we don't compete in the kingdom. If we try to compete, we cut off our own life flow because our brothers and sisters carry what we need and vice versa. We belong to the same body quite literally.

A New Way to Live

We need each other in a new covenant way. No longer do we simply follow lists of rules; instead we are led by the voice of God living inside. Remember, the new law of the Spirit is greater than the old Law because the old Law was a shadow of the new law of the Spirit. That means that the new law is more empowering to us than the old. We have supernatural grace to walk in holiness under the new law.

Man + Law = Human Sweat; Man + Spirit Law = Empowerment

I'll never forget the sudden doubt that hit me as I prepared to minister about the grace and goodness of God. The thought came to me that if the people knew how good God really was, they may live in sin and take advantage of Him. Immediately the Spirit responded to me, *"If I'm sufficient for you, then why do you doubt that I will be sufficient for your brothers and sisters?"* I have never again been afraid to teach fully about the God who I have known all these years.

We don't have to be afraid of teaching about grace and the new law of the Spirit; teaching life cannot cause people to fall back into darkness. The truth is that human sweat cannot inherit the kingdom of God; only spirit inherits Spirit. *"'Not by might nor by power, but by my Spirit,' says the Lord Almighty"* (Zechariah 4:6). If we live by the Spirit we will be empowered by the supernatural God from within. There is not a jot or tittle lost by living by the new law of the Spirit, because all of the commands of God are covered in the new law.

His Happy Presence

If we walk in darkness when we live by the Spirit, we will sense Him crying inside. There is nothing worse than living with a grieving Holy Spirit inside us. It's definitely more fun to sin without Him than with Him, because if we live in rebellion as believers, we constantly feel His aching pain. He doesn't get up and give up on us if we sin; He's not that easy. When He comes inside, He faithfully comes to stay even when it hurts Him.

His happy presence tastes sweeter than anything else in life, and once we have tasted Him no other taste can satisfy. His happy presence becomes the motivating factor in our lives. We don't want to do anything at the expense of His sweet joyful presence.

Knowing Versus Knowing

Gone are the days when father Abraham *told* his child about the living God. Now we *introduce* our children to the living God. No man can teach another to know the Lord by a code or mental knowledge. Now we must know God by our own experience. We must have our own encounters because no longer are we living in the days in which we needed Moses and the priests to tell us what the Lord was like. Now the only way we will *know* Him will be through our own unique experiences with Him.

Spirit + Word of God = Life

The new law of the Spirit doesn't de-emphasize the Bible in our lives, but rather reemphasizes God's Word. The Spirit and the Word of God work together to change and renew us, never contradicting, but always agreeing together to bring us life and truth.

Spirit + Community = Life

Although we have His law of the Spirit living in us, we still need each other because *"You together are that temple"* (1 Corinthians 3:17b). We are intended to walk together in relationship as a corporate ark, each with different strengths and gifts—teaching the Bible, sharing revelation, and encouraging each other to listen and know His voice more. We catch more of Him by simply being in community with each other. There is something about human relationship. When we are in alignment with each other, the magnetic attraction is heightened between heaven and earth.

Mandy Adendorff

Let Your Wineskin Stretch

I Ponder:

When the disciples experienced the filling of the Holy Spirit in Acts 2, they were all together in the same place. Being in the same place is an important factor for heaven to be released to earth. I am not speaking so much of being in the same place physically, but spiritually. You may wonder how it is possible for a group of different people to be in the same place spiritually. It has nothing to do with maturity and everything to do with hunger. When a gathering of people are in the same hungry place, the atmosphere is catching and heaven's fire falls.

Natural hunger exists when there is an empty stomach needing to be filled. A person may fill their hunger with junk food, but their body will eventually reflect malnourishment. So it is in the spiritual: If we believe the lie that He can't fill our hunger, we will fill our lives with other things to avoid disappointment. Spiritual hunger develops when we refuse to ignore our hunger for the real thing. Jesus or bust!

I Realign My Wineskin:

I realign my wineskin by allowing myself to hunger for more of Him, no matter how extreme, even when it feels risky.

I Believe:

God gets immense pleasure from filling my hungry spaces. The bigger my hungry space is, the more God will be able to fill me!

I Activate:

Make the investment to share your life with friends and a community who believe enough to be hungry. Being part of a hungry group of friends will set you up to catch the fire that no one can catch single-handedly.

17. Your Human Touch Brings God's Life

#Godbreathesthroughme

I went through a season when God was teaching me how to preach. One night I had a dream about creating flower arrangements for a wedding. In the dream I was delighted by the berry-like blue flowers spilling in abundance out of the vases. They were unlike any flowers I had ever seen on earth before. Just then a woman with authority came in and was drawn to the arrangements. With an intelligent and critical eye, she noticed some broken pieces and straggly bits hanging from my flowery creations. Suddenly I became shamefully aware that my work was not perfect. The woman took away the live flowers and proceeded to instruct on me how to create flowers from fabric. I tried to create her fake flowers but my usually agile hands became awkward and clumsy. My attempt was ugly and controlled, but most of all, my work lacked life. My heart was disappointed for the bride who I knew would have preferred the living flowers over the safe man-made ones.

God often reminds me to bring life and not perfection, no matter how vulnerable it feels and no matter how much pressure I may feel to fake perfection. Our lives were created when God's breath touched our dust. We are only able to live because we breathe the breath that God imparts. Life has nothing to do with performance. Life exists only in God and human life only happens when dust and heaven mix. Dust is actually part of the equation through which God designed life to flow. He chose to mix the dust of the ground with His breath. He could have chosen gold dust to create our frames, but He chose the simple, beautiful, God-made dust of the earth.

Have you noticed that the handwritten words on a card are far superior to the generic store-bought words? That's because in the imperfect words you can feel the heart, the personality, and the life of the one who sent it to you. Where there is life, there is God. Imperfection is not sin. It shows our humanity and God thinks it's beautiful.

God told Moses in Exodus 25 that the sanctuary being built for Him would be created from yarns, metals, and materials, "from everyone whose heart prompts them to give" (Exodus 25:2b). God didn't zap a perfect sanctuary into existence, but chose to have it made from used materials given in love that had been in transit through the dusty dessert. Even though the materials were recycled, they had great value to God because they came from the heart. They carried life. And He still chooses to live in temples made from dust!

God values you in your rawest state. You don't need to add bells and whistles to impress God or be a life releaser. The uniqueness of your personality, the way you think and express your love and joy—these things are priceless to your Father and valuable to the world. They carry life.

Your life has a personality. The way you love God and the way you express yourself in every way is unique—from your worship to your quirky one-of-a-kind ways. You express God-breathed life into your world. God created you to be human, and your humanity is the chosen container for God's breath. *"We have this treasure in jars of clay to show that this all-surpassing power is from God and not from us"* (2 Corinthians 4:7).

Let Your Wineskin Stretch

I Ponder:

God has created me like no other, and my human qualities are essential to my God-given mission. My humanity will carry the anointing of heaven to my world.

I Realign My Wineskin:

I realign my wineskin by not allowing my mind to compare myself with others. I understand that the life I carry is from God and it has a different personality from the life of another. God will anoint the expression of life that only I can carry.

I Believe:

My human touch is what God loves and people need.

I Activate:

1. Take some time simply *being* with God and feeling His pleasure over you without performing or "doing" anything to earn His pleasure. I like to make myself aware of His pleasure over me when I am doing stuff that is not spiritual, like decorating, shopping, cleaning, driving, etc.

2. Allow yourself to be aware of Him apart from your performance, and enter a new dimension of walking in His presence 24/7.

18. Trustees of Raw Gold

#notafraidtofail

I dreamed of being an artist from my earliest memory. My parents helped me nurture my dream by sacrificing time and money and sending me to a performing arts high school. I came to know Jesus in high school, but later on I also came to know religion.

The sad part is that religion crushed my dream. When it came time to go to college I chose to study art and Bible education for children. I would have loved to study fine art, but that seemed useless to the world and unspiritual. I would also have loved to study pastoral and evangelical ministry, but I was a woman. I crushed the passionate dreams of my Father in me because they were different from the acceptable Christian norms in my circles.

Presence carriers are not called to drop their day jobs and head for the church. Most of us are intended to carry His glory into secular places. We are meant to be the influencers in every sector of society from business and politics to the arts and recreation. His glory is not only reserved for church. We are temples every day in every place.

The Holy Spirit takes any willing person and equips them to be a glory carrier. Remember how Joshua's army had to be the legs for the ark? That army didn't assume they could be lazy and second rate because they had the ark with them. On the contrary, they used whatever they had to be as excellent as they could be to carry God's presence. We too are the legs of His presence. We have each been given our own unique desires and gifts to make us the type of legs needed to bring His presence. Remember it's not Him alone. It could have been all Him if

He chose it to be, but He chose a different way. He chose the "you plus Him" plan.

It's Safe to Excel

"Tall poppy syndrome" describes a social phenomenon in which the tallest most successful poppies in the garden are cut down to equal the size of the rest of the poppies. It is used to describe political and social ideas, but this concept happens in the church too. We shouldn't be afraid to excel in the secular world; we must excel outside church!

We don't have to be afraid to become the best we can be at what we do. How tragic that old wineskin beliefs disdain success among believers. God is waiting for us to explore our gifts and pursue our desires. It is an old wineskin belief that says natural skills and understanding are not valuable. It is God who gave us incredible brains and abilities, not the enemy.

We are intended to sharpen and increase whatever raw materials we have been given. When Jesus spoke of loving God with all our hearts, souls, and minds He meant it. Our mind is a magnificent display of God's creative power. If we do little with it, it will serve us anyway, but if we challenge, educate, and expand it, it will be capable of creating more wonders. Everything God creates is supposed to increase and even create more.

Our brains are a perfect example of this. If we invest in our minds and gifts as heaven's deposits on earth, we will bring a bountiful harvest. Education and learning are kingdom principles that not only bring transformation, but also can bring godly influence into all circles.

Natural skills are a vital part of us because the spiritual and natural work together to release the kingdom. When we mature spiritually and naturally, we will be able to powerfully release the kingdom in wider spheres of influence. God's dreams are bigger than ours; we are safe to keep stretching our dreams and not be considered unspiritual by doing so.

Talented Trustees

I recently heard about a young soldier who had been badly wounded and was recovering in a hospital. The soldier and his family were reeling from pain and loss, but in all of it they were comforted by the amazing nurses and doctors who were caring for them.

God is the giver of special gifts to those in the medical profession. They are gifted so that they can release comfort and healing to multitudes of people. God has not gifted them for themselves, but in His mercy for the people. The nurse is not given a gift of nursing so that she can say, *I'm a nurse*, but so that she can give this gift away to many people. This concept of being a channel for God's gifts to others works in every realm of gifting.

When we think of a person as being gifted we often think how blessed they are, when really we should think of how blessed we are because the gift given to that person is actually given to us by God through a human conduit. When God gives a gift to the world, He uses a person to administer that gift.

When God gives us a gift, no matter what it is, it is given with the purpose of having it released to others. Obviously the trustee, the one who has the gift, is also blessed. It is wonderful to sense the glory of God flowing through us, but the gift is also intended for the multitudes through the trustee.

Let Your Wineskin Stretch

I Ponder:

We are all trustees who have been given gifts to administer in different ways. It is possible to shut up our gifts for multiple reasons. One reason is because we don't think our gift is good enough and it is easier to keep these gifts in the safety of seclusion. In reality your gift is not yours to hold on to or hide; it's yours to mature and sharpen so that you can release it to the many others it was intended for.

I Realign My Wineskin:

I realign my wineskin by thinking the way God thinks about my gifts. I don't focus on how inadequate I feel or how others may view me. Instead I choose to release what God has put inside me as His gift to the world.

I Believe:

I believe God uses people like me to release His gifts to the earth. I realize that my gift may seem small and imperfect, but I believe that every good gift comes from Him and He has entrusted me to release my gifts. I believe that as I release and sow into my gifts, they will increase in me.

I Activate:

1. Ask Holy Spirit to show you if He is highlighting a certain gift within you that He is inviting you to invest in.

2. Step into those gifts by not only releasing the raw gifts from heaven, but by investing time, energy, and resources into sharpening your gifts.

Hint: Often the desire in your heart (no matter how random) is the thing God is stirring you to pursue. One of the Wright brothers (the first to invent aircraft controls that made fixed-wing powered flight possible) had an inner war with himself over his passionate dream for flight. Flight invention seemed like such a frivolous desire for him to pursue as the son of a preacher. Little did he know that he was given this gift as a tool to help advance the gospel. Flight has been one of the most powerful tools in taking the gospel to the uttermost parts of the earth. Your dreams may not seem spiritual enough to you, but take heart. God loves to use unique people with unusual dreams.

19. Light Attracts Treasure

#heaven'streasurehunters

Buried under the surface of the earth are millions of lost living treasures. The treasures are hidden in dirt and unrecognizable, and even they do not understand what they are.

The treasure hunter heroes arrive on the scene sporting an impressive array of picks and shovels. Unfortunately, their efforts at digging and removing dirt cannot reveal the beauty of the treasure. All they are capable of doing is exposing the brokenness and damage of the treasure. These treasures aren't man-made, so man's equipment can't reveal them. The treasure is made from heavenly substance and can only be activated by heaven's methods.

The treasure hunters weep because the treasure is broken and lifeless; their tools and efforts have failed. They put down their picks and shovels and in desperation begin to call out to the treasure. They speak to the motionless objects, telling them who they really are.

At the sound of this strange news, the treasures begin to stir. Something has been awakened, something ancient and supposedly lost forever. They rise up out of the dirt in attraction to the One who calls them treasure.

As they rise up, the earth breaks off them and the ground beneath is disturbed. Other broken treasures begin to feel the movement and change. Something real is happening. Hope arises under the earth and entire sections of land ripple as a domino effect causes countless treasures to awaken and be reclaimed. This parable speaks of the awakening of our generation and reveals keys for releasing the treasure of this age.

God's Riches Are People

Isaiah the prophet tells of a great procession of nations coming to the Lord. *"Nations will come to your light, and kings to the brightness of your dawn"* (Isaiah 60:3). He goes on to describe the people of the nations as the riches of the earth. God's treasures are people—great and small, broken and whole. They are so valuable to God that He gave His own Son to reclaim them.

Once reclaimed, we become the treasure hunters. If we try to find lost treasure by picking away, exposing and trying to remove their sin, they will simply remain broken treasure. Human methods to reclaim lost souls are useless.

Heaven's way is simply to reveal truth. Lost treasures are blind to the truth of who they are and how they are loved. They don't know that they are lost royalty and that their Father still longs for them. Their incredible worth must be revealed to them. This is the truth that they do not know. We are the reconcilers; we are the ones who call out to them and reveal who they are.

New News, Old Gospel

We have been given the ministry of reconciliation. We are called reconcilers—not exposers of sin. In the story of the women caught in adultery, the religious system saw themselves as exposers of sin. They wanted to do God's work by uncovering her sin, which literally brought death.

Jesus used heaven's way and uncovered her treasure instead (even in the glaring reality of her sin) by revealing to the woman that He believed she could be whole. Think about how Jesus responded to the woman for a moment; He spoke a word of forgiveness over her and a charge to live in purity. He revealed to her that He believed she could be a whole person and live a whole life. He believed in her. His words released her to become the woman she never thought she could be. As lost treasure discerns the hope of their new identity they are able to rise up, and sin will lose its grip like dirt falls to the ground.

The ministry of reconciliation calls out to the deepest longing in people and reveals to them who they really are—the treasure of the nations! This is the new, old news, and our lost generation doesn't know this news. This is the original message of the good news; it tells them the best news ever given—the crazy, ridiculous truth that instead of counting their sins against them, God gave Jesus to restore them, His treasure!

As hearts respond to the hope of the *new* news, they are reconciled to God. Reconciled people change, and so does the atmosphere around them. The change can be seen and felt and caught. Whole communities, schools, cities, and nations will be reconciled this way.

Let Your Wineskin Stretch

I Ponder:

The work of two kinds of treasure hunters:

1. Conventional hunters use a pick and shovel to remove the dirt (sin and corruption), but exposing and attempting to remove sin simply reveals hopeless objects. These treasures are not man-made, so man's judgments cannot bring life to them. These are Spirit-made treasures, and they possess heaven-created hearts that can only be activated by heaven's methods.

2. Kingdom hunters understand the only way to release lost treasure—to declare God's heart to them. They must tell them who they really are, God's very passion! When lost treasures understand the hope before them, they will rise from the earth in expectation to meet the One who calls them His treasure. Dirt does not need to be picked off living treasure; it falls off on the journey.

I Realign My Wineskin:

I realign my wineskin by seeing people like God sees them—the riches and wealth of the nations. People are the treasures of the earth who make God's heart faint with desire. Sin is easy to recognize, and most people know their own dirt. When I see with God's eyes, I will see people as God sees them—His lost treasures. I am the voice crying out in the wilderness to the hearts of people to rise up toward the One who loves them.

I Believe:

I have been given the ministry of reconciliation. I am empowered by Him to reconcile treasure to God.

I Activate:

Ask Holy Spirit to reveal treasure about the people around you and take the courage to tell them what God sees. A wonderful, easy form of evangelism is seeing a person the way God sees them and telling them what we see. People are naturally drawn to the way God looks at them. Speaking life to unbelievers is like breathing mouth-to-mouth into a dying person.

"All this is from God, who reconciled us to himself through Christ and gave us the ministry of reconciliation: that God was reconciling the world to himself in Christ, not counting people's sins against them. And he has committed to us the message of reconciliation. We are therefore Christ's ambassadors, as though God were making his appeal through us. We implore you on Christ's behalf: Be reconciled to God. God made him who had no sin to be sin for us, so that in him we might become the righteousness of God" (2 Corinthians 5:18–21).

20. New Clothing

#heaven'sdeposit

As a little girl I loved the feeling of falling asleep on the couch while the family watched late night TV. The best part was later finding myself tucked into my own cuddly bed. My daddy was responsible for that. Death to the believer is like falling asleep in the living room of earth and waking up in the heart of heaven. We will exhale our last breath on earth and instantly we will inhale our next in heaven. No matter how treacherous it may seem, nothing can destroy us. We win!

When we first encountered the Lord Jesus and received Him, we received eternal life. Jesus is eternal life. Eternal life doesn't begin when we die; eternal life begins when we receive Jesus. When Jesus enters us so does His life. Death is not the door to salvation, Jesus is. *"Whoever has the Son has life; whoever does not have the Son of God does not have life. I write these things to you who believe in the name of the Son of God so that you may know that you have eternal life"* (1 John 5:12-13).

Scripture speaks of water baptism being like a death. Baptism is the prophetic act of what has and will happen: We hold our breath as we enter the water. We willfully stop breathing, symbolizing death to the old, and then we are raised up breathing a new life. We have died in the pool of baptism and the life we now live is eternal. Nothing can destroy us. When we finally leave these bodies, we will simply be stepping out of earth into heaven.

God Magnet

Jesus came to destroy the works of the enemy, and death was number one. Death has no more sting for the one who walks through it and finds that it is but a shadow. Yet to loved ones who are left behind, the shadow of death is cruel. The Lord encourages us who are left behind by giving us a seemingly strange promise for ourselves and our loved ones who believe—He promises us a mansion.

What's with the Mansion?

One of the greatest concerns we have about death (especially the death of a loved one) is not where they will live, but what they will become. We are not too concerned if they live in a heavenly apartment or a heavenly mansion, but we are concerned about what happens to their soul. Will they have a body and their mind? Will their spirit float around? (And will they live alone in a big, cold, gold mansion?)

Why would Jesus promise us a mansion when housing is our least concern? God is so good. Jesus gave us this promise to answer our restless questions and put our anxious hearts at rest. I submit to you that when Jesus refers to mansions in heaven, he is referring to our new bodies and minds. The words Jesus chose to comfort us about death are these: *"In my Father's house are many mansions: if it were not so, I would have told you. I go to prepare a place for you"* (John 14:2 NKJV).

We have seen through the Old and New Testament that humans are often referred to as a dwelling of some sort—a tent, a house, or even a temple. The New Testament reveals what happens to us when our earthly bodies die: *"For we know that if the earthly tent we live in is destroyed, we have a building from God, an eternal house in heaven, not built by human hands. Meanwhile we groan, longing to be clothed instead with our heavenly dwelling, because when we are clothed, we will not be found naked. For while we are in this tent, we groan and are burdened, because we do not wish to be unclothed but to be clothed instead with our heavenly dwelling, so that what is mortal may be swallowed up by life. Now the one who has fashioned us for this very purpose is God, who has given us the Spirit as a deposit, guaranteeing what is to come"* (2 Corinthians 5:1–5).

The above Scripture refers to the human body as a tent, a temporary dwelling for our souls to live in. Our tent has a measure of glory; God imparts beauty and brilliance to our human bodies. Our souls experience pleasures through our bodies like sights, sounds, feelings, food; the physical life is glorious, yet a greater glory is coming for our souls to live in—not a lesser glory. Our new bodies are not inferior to our earthly bodies, but eternal.

Living in this tent on earth is like being naked compared to the new bodies which we will receive in heaven. Our earthly tents are vulnerable and need clothes. We have difficulty in this tent, and we long and groan for clothing. Yet our souls will be clothed with a house and not a tent. We will receive our permanent dwelling, a home for our soul. In our new house we will no longer die or be vulnerable, but perfect. God Himself will create our new house.

When we relocate from this tent to our mansion, life will actually swallow up mortality and weakness. There will be no weakness and vulnerability in our new bodies.

After His resurrection Jesus had flesh and bones; He ate food and could move around in an unrestricted capacity. He was not a spirit without a home. We must never fear that our spirits will be without a home. We will not be left to float around the atmosphere. Jesus promised us a new body, a mansion in comparison to our present tents. We have an innate need for a body because God created us to have bodies and He has promised us a superior body, a mansion! When Jesus promises us a mansion, He is comparing our heavenly bodies to our earthly bodies as a mansion would be compared to a tent.

Supernatural Clothing for Our Earthly Tents

In the meantime while we live on earth in our tents, God doesn't leave us naked and vulnerable; instead He clothes us with clothing from heaven.

After Jesus' resurrection He instructs His disciples to wait in Jerusalem for the Holy Spirit, "*I am going to send you what my Father has promised; but stay in the city until you have been clothed with power from on high*" (Luke 24:49). This likens the Spirit to clothing for us while we live in our temporary tents. The Holy Spirit is our source of power that covers our vulnerable tents as we live on earth.

Before Jesus ascended to heaven His disciples asked Him if He was going to restore the kingdom to Israel at that time. They were concerned about their King's authority and power reigning on earth. They felt weak and alone in a hostile world and they wanted to see Israel become a piece of heaven on earth.

Jesus didn't correct their desire or their concept which would come to pass in the Father's time. But Jesus did answer them by revealing how their desire for kingdom dominion would play out in the earth, "*It is not for you to know the times or dates the Father has set by his own authority. But you will receive power when the Holy Spirit comes on you; and you will be my witnesses in Jerusalem, and in all Judea and Samaria, and to the ends of the earth*" (Acts 1:7-8).

He revealed to the disciples that the kingdom would be released to earth, but in a way that their minds had not yet conceived. They would not receive power and authority from a nation, but from heaven. Heaven would become their resource; they would begin a process of receiving from heaven and releasing to earth until the whole world would be covered with His glory.

The Holy Spirit is given to us as a deposit, a guarantee. A guarantee is a down payment, a small percentage of what is to come later. God promises us greater glory in our new bodies and our greater ability to know and contain His glory. In the meantime He gives us a taste of what is coming. The Holy Spirit is our taste and there is so much more to come. (See 2 Corinthians 5:5.)

This reassurance is not given to encourage us to escape from this life. God's heart for us is not to become a reclusive people, waiting to escape and get to heaven. The Holy Spirit's deposit is given to comfort us and give us hope of what is to come, but He is also given to clothe us with heaven now, so that we can release heaven to earth while we live in these bodies.

Let Your Wineskin Stretch

I Ponder:

The deposit of the Holy Spirit and our hope of eternal life are not given to make us forget our earthly life and wait to die. God comforts us by revealing some details of life in our new home. He does this because He doesn't want us to mourn as those without hope. He does not reveal these things to us to make us into a survivalist people who can't wait to get out of here. He calls us to stay and He gives us His Spirit as a deposit to empower us to take dominion. Instead of being buried, this deposit must increase in and through us until the earth is covered with His kingdom glory.

I Realign My Wineskin:

I realign my wineskin by understanding that my purpose in this season is on earth right where I live.

I Believe:

I am called to stay, and I have been clothed on the inside by Holy Spirit who empowers me to stay.

I Activate:

1. Allow yourself to dream, especially if you have experienced a death that makes you want to give up living here. Your dreams release God's life back to you, because God's heart is released through the passions of the heart that is aligned with Him.

2. Do a spirit-pulse test—*I should be dreaming.* Even when Moses was about to die, he was dreaming of the Promised Land. We are never too old to dream, and we are clothed and sealed with Holy Spirit who helps us to dream and activate our dreams!

"And you also were included in Christ when you heard the message of truth, the gospel of your salvation. When you believed, you were

145

marked in him with a seal, the promised Holy Spirit, who is a deposit guaranteeing our inheritance until the redemption of those who are God's possession—to the praise of his glory" (Ephesians 1:13-14).

21. God Unchained

#tagyou'reit

For most of my school days I had a block against Christianity and Christians. I, like so many others, misunderstood so much. In high school I skipped Bible class whenever I could, simply because I didn't have the desire and energy to argue with my teacher anymore. (Bible class was part of the public school curriculum in South Africa.) In elementary school I remember reporting a girl to the teacher for telling me that I was going to hell because I was Jewish. (I don't think she actually said that, but that is how I understood her.) I remember the irritation that burned inside me over a Christian acquaintance because I felt that she was unjust and yet pious at the same time.

And then there was a girl in the ninth grade. She was a quiet girl who I liked, but she didn't say much. One day she spoke in an English speech about being born again. I don't think I listened much, I certainly didn't remember any of her words. But something made an impact on me that day. It wasn't her message, it was her *being*. I sensed love. This young woman embodied the Word of God and I felt it.

Embodying God

There was a time in history when the church kept the Word out of bounds for ordinary people. The ordinary person could not even read the Bible. That was one of our greatest failures. God's Word was locked up in church. Thank God for the heroes of the day who laid down their lives to make God's Word accessible to people again.

147

God Magnet

Jesus is the Word made flesh. His mission was to make the Word accessible to ordinary people. Jesus made Himself available to everyone; not only did He invite the ordinary guys to come to Him, but he found creative ways to reveal God. His revealing of God didn't look anything like what modern Judaism had become. His creativity, lack of performance, and authenticity gripped the multitudes but challenged the religious. He clearly wanted to bring heaven in a way that earth could grasp.

We have become the new ark, the temple, and the gateway for God to encounter mankind. But it is still possible to lock the Word up in a temple. Though our goal is to make God's love accessible, it is possible to unknowingly create stumbling blocks instead of stepping-stones for people.

Our mission is the same today as it was for Jesus: To make the Word flesh, to make God accessible and to be a gate for heaven to flow through. Jesus did everything possible to make heaven accessible to folk. He ministered in unconventional ways by telling gripping stories, healing sick people (often in quite creative ways), showing kindness, and honoring people. He broke through mental blocks and walls by simply revealing God in ways that mattered to average folk. He didn't focus on the jots and tittles, but on the stuff that people could relate to. It is wisdom for us to remove the stumbling blocks that often seem normal in Christian circles, but are simply cultural, performance-driven, or traditional in nature. If a person chooses to stumble, let it only be on Jesus and the kingdom.

On the Wings of Creativity and Innovation

I lived in South Africa when the apartheid regime came down. For the first time black children were allowed to attend white schools. During this season I had a great opportunity to minister in some of the public schools. I was happy to have open doors, but the students were so broken and disenchanted by "white religion" that they struggled to receive from me. Many students came during recess to sit in the class, but there was a block. These children had grown up in the oppressive apartheid system. Christianity was tainted with oppression because the apartheid was powered by warped church ideology. On the first day that I stood in the classroom with my Jesus, I represented pain and injustice to them. My words seemed very flat. I had remembered being in a similar place as them only a few years before, and it was then that I came up with the idea to paint for them.

The following week I began my experiment. I brought in a large board and painted to music. Something remarkable happened—everyone in the room became captivated and hungry to receive something from God. There are many reasons why creativity changes the atmosphere. In this situation creativity broke the mold of the Christianity to which they had been exposed. Also, the mere process of creating in front of them made me vulnerable, like them. But most of all they were rocked by what they felt. They sensed God's presence.

This is how my art ministry began. It began simply as a makeshift experiment to communicate love through racial pain and mistrust. I had no idea art could be such a powerful tool. I didn't realize that anyone else had ever done such a strange thing before; it was only years later that I discovered that many others in the kingdom were also using art to minister in a myriad of ways. But the arts are only one small facet of creativity; and contrary to popular belief, creativity is not confined to the right-brained sector of society. God is Creator and every *creat*ure has the ability to create in their identity and DNA. Creativity is the fingerprint of God on humanity.

Creativity: The Language of Heaven and Human

Creativity will flourish and expand in the new wineskin just like new wine does! Our imaginations were created to be the birthplace of this creativity. Both imagination and creativity are good and perfect gifts given to humanity to enjoy and increase. All people in all cultures of all faiths respond to creativity and new things. It's the language of heaven and human. The message of the kingdom can be carried far and wide on the wings of creativity.

Where there is creativity there is change. Change is not always easy. We need stretchable wineskins to accommodate change. But if we don't sense the ever-moving rhythms of heaven and create new sounds, media, and culture, we will fail to bring the increase of God's kingdom. If we fail on our watch then our children will have to fight for a renaissance from a dark age. God wants to impart new ways for us to release heaven and it may not look very spiritual, because often these ideas come through very natural expressions.

Risky Business

Creativity is always an experiment and a risk. If we're looking for a foolproof, sure plan to grow in church attendance then we'd better stick with the old model. But if our goal is to take territory not yet taken, we will have to walk in uncharted territory, which means every day will be an experiment and a risk. There is no hero who didn't experiment and take huge risks. And there is no hero who didn't pick up some strange looks along the way. If we keep singing the safe songs, painting the usual way, and operating in the normal church model we will never fail, but we will also never lead.

Creativity Is Faith

The good news is that creativity is not a special gift. It's true that some people have special skills and gifts, but creativity is a mindset. Artists are usually the most creative people because their skill set gives them a space to grow in the area of creativity, but creativity is not just reserved for the chosen.

I know left-brained business people who are more creative than many artists. Creativity is not about the skill; it's about pushing into new territory and experimenting. You can be highly creative in any field— from raising kids to designing governmental structures. Creativity is simply the faith to attempt something that comes from the imagination. And creativity has the grace to keep experimenting through criticism and failure.

The early church was an experiment. The leaders didn't know as much as we think they knew; they learned as they went along. There were times when senior leaders argued over possible change, and thankfully change won (see Acts 15:6–12). There were times when they had to learn innovative and new ways to present the gospel (see Acts 17:22-23). Thankfully Paul didn't have a formula to stick to. There were times when they had to institute offices never before given in the church (see Acts 6:1–6). Thankfully they were ready to try some new solutions. This change and experimentation should always be on the increase or we need to check our pulse. If the kingdom is increasing under our feet we will be moving into new places and continual change will be normal and expected.

Where there is increase there will always be creativity. And where there is creativity, there will always be messes and failures. It's a good day when we finally understand that performance has no more place in our lives, families, and churches, because that will be the day when we choose destiny above success.

Let Your Wineskin Stretch

I Ponder:

The secret of God's dream that was hidden for generations has now been revealed to us—God Himself will live in us. The Holy Spirit lives in me and He has invested in me the hope of the nations. All of heaven and the cloud of witnesses watch my life in anticipation.

I Realign My Wineskin:

Think about the fact that the Bible is true. God really does live in you. Imagine that your dreams and imaginations are really ideas from His heart. Imagine that these ideas are wings to carry a new sound, a new voice, a new design, a new business model, a new something with the DNA of heaven that will be like the bottle of milk for the lost lambs. Imagine that you can actually believe enough to take the risk and do it.

I Believe:

Every time I make myself vulnerable enough to release my love and my life, I give Jesus another chance to breathe on earth through human flesh.

I Activate:

Tag—you're it!

"The mystery which has been hidden from ages and from generations, but now has been revealed to His saints. To them God willed to make known what are the riches of the glory of this mystery among the Gentiles: which is Christ in you, the hope of glory" (Colossians 1:26-27 NKJV).

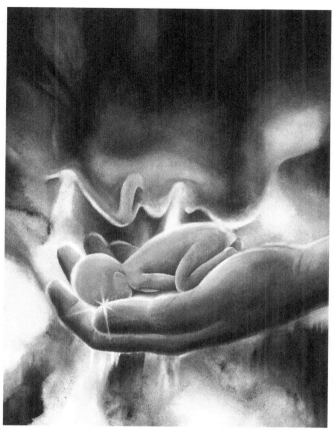

Painting by Mandy Adendorff

Receive a gift from Mandy's Studio.

"Color for Your Day" is Mandy's weekly e-mail that combines her inspiring art with a fresh word for your encouragement.

Subscribe for free by going to www.mandyadendorff.com.

For events and information regarding Mandy Adendorff's schedule, visit www.mandyadendorff.com or www.godmagnet.com.

About the Author

Mandy Adendorff is an award-winning artist and an itinerant preacher; she began her walk of faith after having a secret encounter with Messiah as a Jewish teenager. In 1993 Mandy began a ministry that combines live art and speaking to reach broken youth of South Africa. It has been more than twenty years and Mandy is still ministering the kingdom. Mandy and her husband, Stuart, have two adult daughters and live in beautiful New England, USA where Mandy's ministry and art studio is based.

We are a Christian media company dedicated to:

Documenting God's supernatural ability on the earth and devoting our lives to understanding the international trade standard publishing industry in order to cultivate wisdom in writing.

Discover more at www.5FoldMedia.com.